BOURBON WHISKEY I
RC 53 G
04-14-17
FILL DATE: 17-D-14
LOT NO
FILL DATE:
LOT NO
RESERVE DISTILLERY
DSP-KY-52
RC 53
CHINKAPIN
FILL DATE 06-16-16
LOT NO. 16-F-16
WOODFORD RESERVE

The WHISKEY COOKBOOK

THE WHISKEY COOKBOOK

13-Digit ISBN: 978-1-64643-320-9
10-Digit ISBN: 1-64643-320-3

This book may be ordered by mail from the publisher. Please include $5.99 for postage and handling. Please support your local bookseller first!

Books published by Cider Mill Press Book Publishers are available at special discounts for bulk purchases in the United States by corporations, institutions, and other organizations. For more information, please contact the publisher.

Cider Mill Press Book Publishers
"Where good books are ready for press"
PO Box 454
12 Spring Street
Kennebunkport, Maine 04046

Visit us online!
cidermillpress.com

Typography: Brix Slab, Modesto, Trade Gothic

Pages 18–19, 20, 26–27, 30–31, 35, 36,39–40, 50, 62–63, 76, 79, 86–87, 96–97, 102–103, 122, 128–129, 154, 161, 169, 180–181, 190–191, 195, 202, 207, 220–221, 228, 238–239, 250–251, and 258–259 courtesy of Cider Mill Press. Page 38 courtesy of Heather Wibbels. Pages 61, 177, 208, and 224 courtesy of StockFood. Pages 64, 130, 151, 204, and 211 courtesy of Michter's Distillery. Pages 107, 109, 110, 113,114–115, 118, 201, and 231 courtesy of the Intercontinental Hotel, Barcelona. Page 158 courtesy of Stan Lee. Page 162 courtesy of Erica Drum. Page 179 courtesy of Bardstown Bourbon Company. All other images used under official license from Shutterstock.com.

Printed in China
Back cover image: Irish Whiskey-Glazed Ribs, see page 163
Front endpaper image: Creamy Scotch & Mushroom Sauce, see page 148
Back endpaper image: Sweet & Spicy Honey Glaze, see page 133

1 2 3 4 5 6 7 8 9 0
First Edition

The
WHISKEY
COOKBOOK

SENSATIONAL TASTING NOTES AND PAIRINGS FOR BOURBON, RYE, SCOTCH, AND SINGLE MALTS

RICHARD THOMAS

CIDER MILL PRESS

BOOK PUBLISHERS

KENNEBUNKPORT, MAINE

CONTENTS

INTRODUCTION

When it came to food pairings, wine used to be the only game in town. At first, the job of suggesting wine-and-food pairings fell to the wine waiter. This led to the development of a new role in fine dining establishments: the sommelier. Much of the professional infrastructure surrounding this trade (certifications, associations, etc.) only came to be between the late 1960s and early 1980s. It's no coincidence that the decade in the middle of that establishment era—the 1970s—saw the wine world start to take American and other New World wines seriously. During this decade, changing tastes in the West pushed wine to the top of the drinks mountain.

Coincidentally, that decade also saw the World Whiskey Bust, as those aforementioned changing tastes carried people away from brown spirits, sending whiskey makers from Aberdeen, Scotland, to Bardstown, Kentucky, into their own industry-specific economic Depression.

Wine pairings became an institution because Boomers generally weren't all that interested in other drinks when they went out to eat at nice restaurants. But the idea of curated pairings of food with other kinds of drinks has always been a sound one. Its tendrils sprouted and reached out just as soon as other drink scenes worthy of exploring began to pop up: first with craft beer in the late 1990s, and then the revival of popular interest in bourbon and Scotch in the mid-2000s.

Nowadays, whiskey-and-food pairings are a routine fixture of most industry events, even if it is just in the carefully considered choice of who gets hired to cater an event and the resulting menu selections. Restaurants that want to highlight the whiskey selection at their bar often have recommendations to make, just as they do with wine.

Whiskey enthusiasts also take a stab at curating pairings when entertaining and hosting tastings at home, which also often calls for said enthusiasts to up their cooking game. And that's where a book like this one becomes important: we will be telling you not just how to make pairing suggestions, but also how to make the food that goes with them.

COMPLEMENT OR CONTRAST?

The only ironclad rule of a pairing is that one component should never overwhelm or dominate the other. If you want a single-malt Scotch or bourbon to drink with your medium-rare porterhouse, that whiskey needs to be robust and full-bodied. Likewise, sea bass sashimi is so delicate that one isn't even supposed to dip it in soy sauce, so that delicacy calls for a lighter and more subtle whiskey.

Keeping that rule in mind, the first consideration is whether to complement or contrast in a given pairing or whole slate of them. This topic has something of a heated debate swirling around it. Most I've spoken to on the matter recognize the pros and cons of complementing and/or contrasting. But there are partisans who believe that drink pairings should only complement food, and never contrast it.

The idea behind complementing is to select the flavor profiles that mirror each other. For instance, to complement a spicy, herb-filled dish, reach for a bold, spicy rye like Dad's Hat. The downside of this approach is that, by failing to present some distinctive variety in the menu, it could lead to a bored palate. I also think relying solely on complementary pairings doesn't allow one to showcase their imagination the way that contrasting pairings do.

Andrew Zimmern once said, "All great food is made of contrasts," and the same can be said of food-and-whiskey pairings. The downside of taking this route is the same point as its virtue, however: making successful contrasts requires a good deal of imagination. Furthermore, making contrasts is not something one should simply throw out there. Dialing in contrasting pairings often requires ample preparation and experimentation, which consumes a lot of time and resources. Note that contrasting does not mean veering hard toward the opposite flavor of the food you're pairing with. The point is to stimulate a response, not shock the taste buds.

As an example, one time I served carne asada tacos for a weekend lunch gathering and took both approaches by setting out two bottles of whiskey. The complementary bottle was Maker's Mark, and the contrasting one was Loch Lomond Single Grain. The bourbon was as robust as the beef. As a wheated bourbon, its floral nature proved well suited to the citrus juices used to marinate the meat. As for the Loch Lomond, a Scotch fan probably would not have chosen a light, green apple and grass-driven grain whisky to go with carne asada, but it managed to bring out the best qualities in both the meat and the vegetable and cheese toppings.

WHISKEYS AND THE FLAVORS FOUND THEREIN

The trick to being a sommelier, spirits steward, or ace mixologist, of course, is having an encyclopedic knowledge of what makes each bottle distinctive in its own right. That knowledge is the foundation of choosing what bottle to pair with what food. Though the various tweaks one can make in the production process of any whiskey defies broad generalizations, this book is about combining flavors, and that process needs to start somewhere. So, here is what to expect from the four types of whiskey referenced most often in this book:

Bourbon Whiskey is best known for its caramel, oak, and vanilla flavors, but within those general qualities exist major distinctions.

Irish Whiskey is best known for its light and mellow character, especially compared to the whiskies produced by its neighbor in Scotland. Ireland's whiskeys are usually fruity, accented with vanilla.

Rye Whiskey is distinct from bourbon in that it is based squarely on rye grain instead of corn. Both are aged in new oak barrels, so both have the same current of vanilla running through them. Where rye differs from bourbon is that it is spicy instead of sweet.

Scotch Whisky has the broadest palette of flavors to draw upon of any spirit by far, and perhaps any alcoholic beverage, period. This is a category that runs from modestly grassy and honeyed to saline and as smoky as a crusty chimney; from endowed with light, subtle sherry influences to rich, liquified Black Forest cake. Scotch doesn't lend itself to being pigeonholed. That said, the flavors you will most often find in Scotch are fruit, honey, smoke, and vanilla.

APERITIFS, DIGESTIFS, AND DESSERT WHISKEYS

Long before wine pairings became a thing in the late twentieth century, there was a custom of drinks served before and after dinner, aka aperitifs and digestifs. Although these drinks were consumed separate from the meal, while pairings are meant to be taken with the meal, these offerings provide some helpful concepts to remember when making pairings. Moreover, there is no reason why you cannot use the aperitif-and-digestif approach in place of direct pairings, especially in cases where the meal shares a common theme, or you want to offer beverages other than whiskey alongside the food.

Aperitifs are intended to be served with the appetizers, enjoyed away from the table, and thus function as a separate, minipairing outside of the proper meal. Champagne, cocktails, and sherry are traditional choices for an aperitif, so a whiskey-based cocktail neatly fits this niche.

Strong spirits, such as whiskey, served neat are traditionally frowned upon in the aperitif space because it is believed that they are too strong, overpower the taste buds, and thus fail to stimulate the palate. The logic behind this is similar to why you wouldn't pair any drink except milk with something coated in Da Bomb Beyond Insanity Hot Sauce; you won't be tasting anything—literally—after such a high-wattage encounter.

Cask-strength whiskeys are a poor choice for most pairings, as their sheer potency violates the rule of not overpowering the food. Still, the very existence of a whiskey and food–pairing culture disproves the notion that all whiskeys will batter one's taste buds. Furthermore, if it is deemed necessary to reduce the alcohol strength, there is no reason why whiskey cannot be cut with a splash of water or put on the rocks.

The intent for a digestif is to wind down after a meal and use strong alcohol to aid digestion. Brandy, Cognac, and Port are the most traditional choices for this round of drinks, but sweeter whiskeys are almost as common a choice, and have been for more than a century. Here, at the end, is where the cask-strength stuff should come out, if it is going to appear at all.

Digestifs lead into whiskey as a liquid dessert or as a substitute for dessert wines. Since the choice here should be as sweet as possible, solid options are double new oak bourbon (which augments the vanilla flavor drawn from new oak aging), like Woodford Reserve Double Oaked, or sherry-bomb single-malts, like The Glenlivet Nadurra Oloroso or Aberlour A'Bunadh.

COOKING WITH WHISKEY AND PAIRINGS

Cooks have used wine as an ingredient for millennia, but it's only recently that the idea of using whiskey in recipes has truly caught on and stuck. The idea works much the same way as it does in civet de lapin (rabbit stew with red wine) or beer-battered fish: the alcohol boils away, but the flavor remains. In this respect, if you are using the right whiskey as an ingredient, the accompaniment is already there in the food. If you want to take a step further in that direction, the right whiskey pairing is already spelled out: just use the one that you prepared the dish with.

BRUNCH

Although I don't encourage drinking alcohol, let alone strong alcohol, first thing in the morning, the flavors found in whiskey—American whiskeys in particular—go with the sweet and savory mix found in traditional breakfast foods in a way no other drink can claim. This is amply demonstrated by the now ubiquitous bourbon-and-rye barrel-aged maple syrups on shelves at the market. Beer being "the breakfast of champions" is a joke for a reason, and sparkling offerings are the only wines commonly found at the modern breakfast table.

Only an ambitious alcoholic or wannabe dyspeptic would set a bottle of bourbon on the table at 7 o'clock in the morning, but this doesn't make breakfast whiskey pairings problematic, because of brunch. That later starting time brings the thought of a drink into far more reasonable territory. And, as you'll see once you open your mind, the heartier the breakfast dish, the more a glass of neat whiskey will suit it better than a cocktail. Taking your cue from there, don't hesitate to borrow from Homer Simpson's playbook, and thank God when breakfast becomes dinner. The issue is not with the food, but the time of day. Once you get that sorted, whiskey and breakfast dishes go beautifully together.

12 asparagus spears

3 tablespoons extra-virgin olive oil

Salt, to taste

¾ lb. cooked ham, sliced thin

12 large eggs

6 English muffins, halved

½ cup unsalted butter

4 egg yolks

1½ tablespoons fresh lemon juice

½ cup heavy cream

¼ cup Garrison Brothers bourbon

2 teaspoons Dijon mustard

YIELD: **6 SERVINGS**

ACTIVE TIME: **45 MINUTES**

TOTAL TIME: **1 HOUR**

COURTESY OF GARRISON BROTHERS DISTILLERY

BOURBON EGGS BENEDICT

A bourbon-spiked hollandaise will stretch your Sunday brunch out beautifully.

1. Preheat the oven to 350°F and bring water to a boil in a large saucepan.

2. Place the asparagus in a baking dish, drizzle 2 tablespoons of the olive oil over the top, and toss to coat. Season the asparagus with salt, place it in the oven, and roast until it is browned and tender, 10 to 15 minutes, stirring once or twice. Remove the asparagus from the oven and set it aside.

3. While the asparagus is in the oven, place the remaining olive oil in a skillet and warm it over medium-high heat. Place the ham in the pan and cook until it is warmed through, stirring occasionally, 3 to 4 minutes. Transfer the ham to a platter, cover it with aluminum foil, and set it aside.

4. Working in batches, crack the eggs into a teacup or small, shallow bowl and slip them into the boiling water. Poach the eggs until the whites are set, 4 to 5 minutes. Transfer the cooked eggs to a platter and cover them with aluminum foil.

5. Place the English muffins in a toaster and toast until they are golden brown.

6. While the English muffins are in the toaster, place the butter in a microwave-safe bowl and microwave on medium until it is melted, about 30 seconds. Let the butter cool to room temperature for a few minutes.

7. Whisk the egg yolks, lemon juice, and heavy cream into the melted butter. Place the bowl in the microwave and microwave on medium for 2 minutes, stopping to whisk the mixture every 20 seconds.

8. Remove the sauce from the microwave, add the bourbon and mustard, and whisk until incorporated. Season the sauce with salt and then assemble the eggs Benedict, topping the toasted English muffins with some of the ham, asparagus, and poached eggs. Drizzle the sauce over each portion and enjoy.

YIELD: **8 SERVINGS**
ACTIVE TIME: **15 MINUTES**
TOTAL TIME: **15 MINUTES**

COURTESY OF GARRISON BROTHERS DISTILLERY

MAPLE BOURBON SAUSAGES

Maple and bourbon were made for one another, and smoky sausage completes the hat trick.

¼ cup water

16 breakfast sausage links

2 tablespoons orange marmalade

2 tablespoons maple syrup

1 tablespoon unsalted butter

2 tablespoons Garrison Brothers Small Batch Bourbon

1. Place the water in a large skillet and warm it over medium-high heat. Add the sausages and cook until the water has evaporated and the sausages are nearly cooked through, about 6 minutes.

2. Stir in the marmalade, syrup, and butter and cook until the sausages are evenly coated and entirely cooked through, about 1 minute.

3. Remove the pan from heat, stir in the bourbon, and serve.

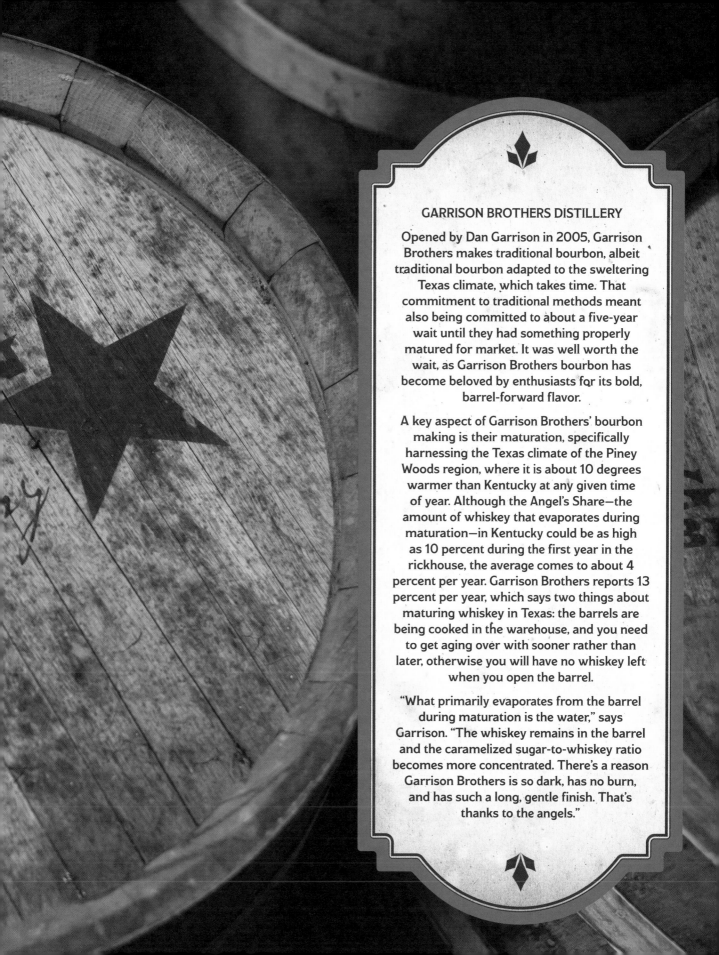

GARRISON BROTHERS DISTILLERY

Opened by Dan Garrison in 2005, Garrison Brothers makes traditional bourbon, albeit traditional bourbon adapted to the sweltering Texas climate, which takes time. That commitment to traditional methods meant also being committed to about a five-year wait until they had something properly matured for market. It was well worth the wait, as Garrison Brothers bourbon has become beloved by enthusiasts for its bold, barrel-forward flavor.

A key aspect of Garrison Brothers' bourbon making is their maturation, specifically harnessing the Texas climate of the Piney Woods region, where it is about 10 degrees warmer than Kentucky at any given time of year. Although the Angel's Share—the amount of whiskey that evaporates during maturation—in Kentucky could be as high as 10 percent during the first year in the rickhouse, the average comes to about 4 percent per year. Garrison Brothers reports 13 percent per year, which says two things about maturing whiskey in Texas: the barrels are being cooked in the warehouse, and you need to get aging over with sooner rather than later, otherwise you will have no whiskey left when you open the barrel.

"What primarily evaporates from the barrel during maturation is the water," says Garrison. "The whiskey remains in the barrel and the caramelized sugar-to-whiskey ratio becomes more concentrated. There's a reason Garrison Brothers is so dark, has no burn, and has such a long, gentle finish. That's thanks to the angels."

YIELD: **6 SERVINGS**

ACTIVE TIME: **30 MINUTES**

TOTAL TIME: **30 MINUTES**

CROISSANT FRENCH TOAST

Buttery croissants make for an elevated French toast.

¾ cup Garrison Brothers Small Batch Bourbon

10 large eggs

2 cups heavy cream

2 tablespoons cinnamon

½ teaspoon freshly grated nutmeg

1 cup maple syrup

2 tablespoons unsalted butter, plus more as needed

8 croissants

Fresh berries, for serving

1. Preheat the oven to 200°F. Place ½ cup of bourbon, the eggs, heavy cream, cinnamon, and nutmeg in a mixing bowl and whisk to combine. In a separate bowl, whisk together the maple syrup and remaining bourbon.

2. Place the butter in a large skillet and melt it over medium heat.

3. Working in batches to avoid crowding the pan, dip the croissants in the batter until they are coated and then place them in the pan. Cook until browned on both sides, about 10 minutes, turning them over just once. Transfer the cooked croissants to a platter and place it in the oven to keep the croissants warm. If the skillet starts to look dry, add butter as needed.

4. When all of the croissants have been cooked, serve them with the bourbon-infused syrup and fresh berries.

BOURBON, MAPLE & BLACK PEPPER BACON, SEE PAGE 34

YIELD: **6 SERVINGS**

ACTIVE TIME: **10 MINUTES**

TOTAL TIME: **1 HOUR AND 45 MINUTES**

COURTESY OF MICHTER'S DISTILLERY

BOURBON, MAPLE & BLACK PEPPER BACON

Keep in mind that the preparation time is the bare minimum—the longer you can let this bacon marinate in the refrigerator, the better the results.

½ lb. bacon, halved crosswise

2 teaspoons coarsely ground black pepper

3 tablespoons Michter's US*1 bourbon

3 tablespoons maple syrup

1. Place all of the ingredients in a resealable plastic bag and toss until the bacon is evenly coated. Place the bacon in the refrigerator and let it marinate for at least 1 hour, and up to 24 hours.

2. Preheat the oven to 375°F and line a baking sheet with aluminum foil. Remove the bacon from the marinade and shake it to remove any excess. Place the bacon on the baking sheet in a single layer and place it in the oven.

3. Cook the bacon until it is crispy and caramelized, 25 to 30 minutes, turning it over as necessary. Remove the bacon from the oven and let it cool slightly on a wire rack before enjoying.

MICHTER'S DISTILLERY

The new iteration of Michter's—a previous outfit under that name had existed in Pennsylvania until the late 1980s—began to take shape in the '90s, a process that included a move to the unofficial capital of American whiskey, Louisville, Kentucky. With help from Brown-Forman veteran Willie Pratt, the company acquired some excellent Kentucky whiskey stock, and began bottling and releasing whiskeys in 2000.

They opened their distillery in Shively in 2015, and in so doing became a middleweight fixture among the big Kentucky distillers. With the opening of their own distillery, Michter's began a period of transition from sourced and contract-produced whiskey to whiskey made in their own house.

WIGLE WHISKEY DISTILLERY

Pitttsburgh's Wigle Distillery plucked its theme out of western Pennsylvania's Whiskey Rebellion, which rumbled from 1791 to 1794. A local farmer and distiller named Phillip Wigle punched out a tax collector, which was reputed to be the first violent act of the rebellion. Wigle was later convicted of treason and sentenced to meet a traitor's death at the gallows, but seeing as how Wigle was a tax evader and not a traitor, President Washington later pardoned him.

This is a craft distillery that is especially keen on its yeasts, drawing on a wide variety of sources, following much experimentation. Co-founder Alex Grelli says they use "Bretanomyces, Belgian yeast strains, yeast slurries from local breweries, malt whiskey yeasts, and spontaneous fermentation from endogenous yeast." They also put a premium on using organic grains grown within 250 miles of the distillery.

YIELD: **1 SERVING**

ACTIVE TIME: **45 MINUTES**

TOTAL TIME: **1 HOUR**

COURTESY OF CHEF ALEX BROWN
FOR WIGLE WHISKEY DISTILLERY

THE BREAKFAST CLUB

The spice from the mustard and horseradish is a great match for the ample spice in Wigle's rye.

For the Port Rye Aioli

1 cup Duke's Mayonnaise

1 tablespoon mashed roasted garlic

2 oz. Wigle Port Rye Whiskey

2 tablespoons prepared horseradish

1 tablespoon Dijon mustard

Salt and pepper, to taste

For the Sandwich

3 slices of potato bread, toasted

2 slices of fresh heirloom tomato

2 legs of Duck Confit (see page 234), bones and skin removed, warmed

3 slices of crispy applewood-smoked bacon

Mixed greens, to taste

1. To prepare the aioli, place all of the ingredients in a mixing bowl and stir until well combined. Taste, adjust the seasoning as necessary, and set the aioli aside.

2. To prepare the sandwiches, spread some aioli on the slices of bread. Arrange the tomato and duck confit on a slice of bread, top with another slice, and layer the greens and bacon on top. Place remaining slice of bread on top of the bacon and enjoy.

YIELD: **1 DRINK**

ACTIVE TIME: **2 MINUTES**

TOTAL TIME: **2 MINUTES**

COURTESY OF AUTHOR, BLOGGER, AND EXECUTIVE BOURBON STEWARD HEATHER WIBBELS, AKA THE COCKTAIL CONTESSA

THE BREKKIE OLD FASHIONED

"The Old Fashioned is one of the oldest cocktails and was originally a morning cocktail. Whiskey and bitters were considered medicinal, and you'd take them each morning the way we take our vitamins today. Much like the Mimosa or Bloody Mary today, it was the cocktail to get you ready to face the day. It's sad that's no longer our tradition because I'd start the day with an Old Fashioned over a Mimosa any day," says Wibbels.

2 oz. Old Forester 86 bourbon

½ oz. Coffee-Infused Maple Syrup (see sidebar)

2 dashes of orange bitters

¼ oz. coffee liqueur (optional)

1 strip of orange zest, for garnish

1. Place all of the ingredients, except for the garnish, in a mixing glass and fill it two-thirds of the way with ice. Stir until the drink is well chilled, about 30 seconds.

2. Strain the cocktail over one large ice cube into a rocks glass. Express the strip of orange zest over the cocktail and then use it as garnish.

COFFEE-INFUSED MAPLE SYRUP

Place 1 cup maple syrup in a saucepan and warm it over medium heat until it is steaming, just before it comes to a simmer. Add 2 table-spoons of dark roast coffee beans and stir for 1 minute. Turn off the heat and let the mixture steep until the coffee flavor is to your liking, 1½ to 2 hours. Strain before using or storing in the refrigerator.

Old Forester is just one of the distilleries that fall under the giant umbrella of Brown-Forman. Brown-Forman's world headquarters, which resembles the campus of a small liberal arts college, is located in Louisville, Kentucky, although no longer in downtown. While several of its major brands, like Woodford and Jack Daniel's, have their own distilleries, the company's massive plant is the engine that drives the Brown-Forman machine.

Old Forester, the oldest and longest running bottled whiskey in America, has been made there for years. From 1920 to 1933, Old Forester was one of only 10 whiskey brands authorized for medicinal purposes, which is why it survived Prohibition.

As Old Forester and Woodford Reserve share a master distiller, the legendary Chris Morris, their bourbons also share a mash bill (72% corn, 18% rye, and 10% malted barley). As you might expect, this relatively high rye component provides Old Forester's whiskeys with a spicy finish that makes their products easy to use in complementary or contrasting pairings.

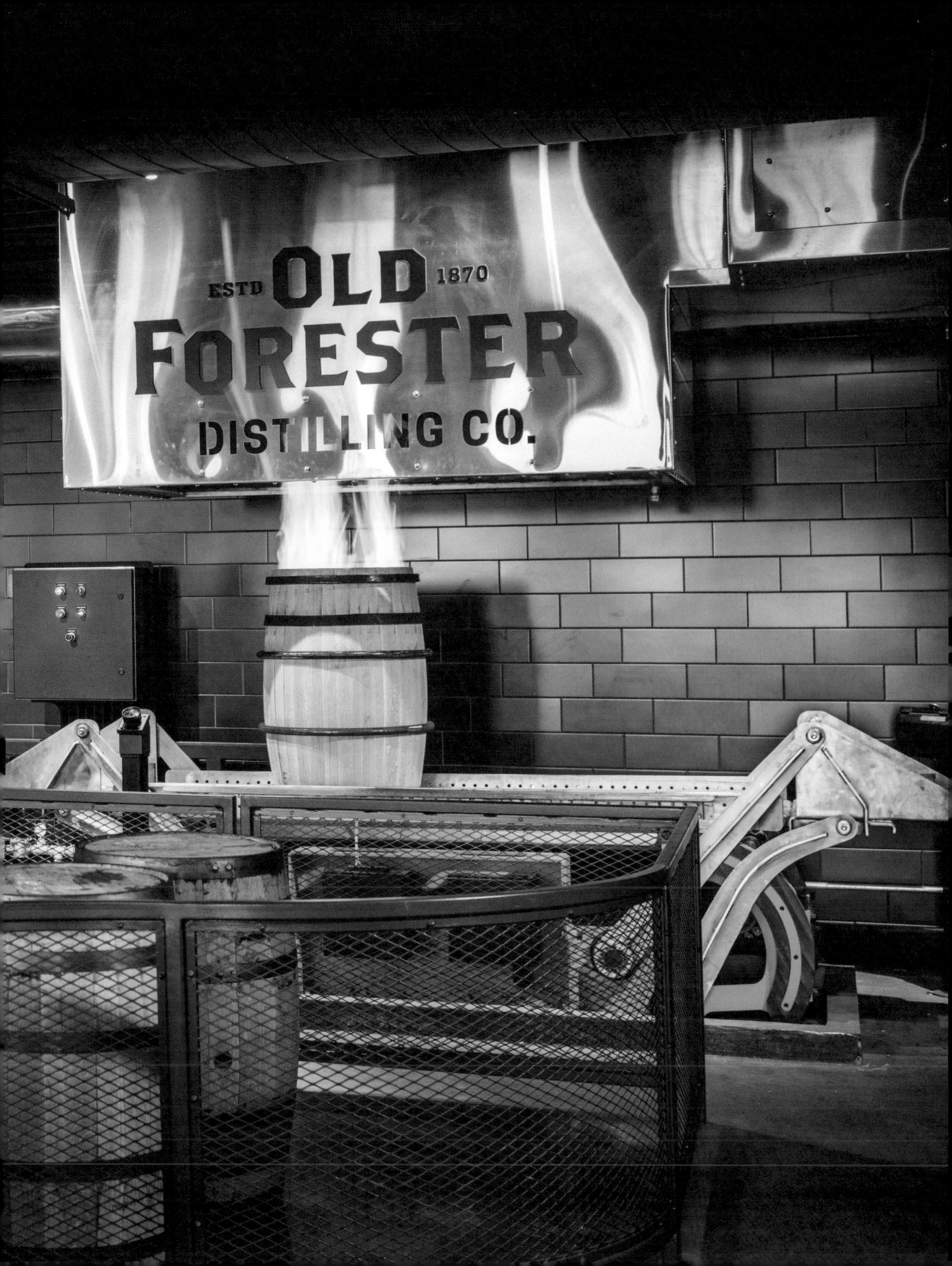
ESTD OLD 1870
FORESTER
DISTILLING CO.

YIELD: **2 TO 4 SERVINGS**

ACTIVE TIME: **10 MINUTES**

TOTAL TIME: **1 HOUR AND 10 MINUTES**

COURTESY OF TAMARA WAGNER

AVOCADO & CUCUMBER SOUP

Soups and stews are probably not the first thing to come to mind for tastings and pairings with whiskeys, but that notion is flawed. If the setting for the pairings is a three-or-more course meal, often the affair will begin with a small bowl of soup. In these instances, the soup course gets a pairing, too, as I have experienced many times. In a humbler setting, it is common to turn to a warming bowl of soup or a stimulating pour of whiskey to alleviate winter chills, and, of course, the best move of all is to put them together. Pair this crisp yet creamy soup with the Mackmyra Svensk Rök Swedish Single Malt. Pairing with Svensk Rök straddles the line between contrast and complement, as the malt was smoked with juniper berries.

½ cucumber, rinsed well and diced

Flesh of ½ avocado

Zest and juice of ½ lemon (organic recommended)

1 cup Vegetable Stock (see page 248)

Salt and pepper, to taste

Fresh chives, chopped, for garnish

1. Place the cucumber, avocado, lemon zest, lemon juice, and stock in a blender and puree until smooth.

2. Season the soup with salt and pepper and chill in the refrigerator for at least 1 hour before serving. Garnish with chives and enjoy.

BLOODY MARY GAZPACHO

Don't hesitate to dress this soup up with your preferred Bloody Mary accompaniments.

¼ cup Garrison Brothers bourbon

6 cups Bloody Mary mix

4 cups chopped tomatoes

1½ cups finely diced cucumber

¼ cup yellow bell pepper

¼ cup finely diced red onion

¼ cup fresh lemon juice

2 garlic cloves, minced

Salt and pepper, to taste

Fresh basil, chiffonade, for garnish

1. Place the bourbon, Bloody Mary mix, tomatoes, cucumber, bell pepper, red onion, lemon juice, and garlic in a large mixing bowl and stir to combine.

2. Season the soup with salt and pepper, ladle it into chilled bowls, and garnish each portion with basil.

YIELD: **24 MUFFINS**

ACTIVE TIME: **10 MINUTES**

TOTAL TIME: **1 HOUR**

CORN MUFFINS

If you want a little more flavor in these muffins, sauté half of a finely diced onion and 4 minced jalapeño peppers, and add them with the sour cream. New Southern Revival's 100% Jimmy Red Corn Bourbon, with its creamy sweetness, makes a wonderful pairing for these.

1 lb. unsalted butter

14 oz. sugar

9 eggs

2 lbs. sour cream

15 oz. white cornmeal

12 oz. cake flour

1 oz. baking powder

1 tablespoon fine sea salt

1. Preheat the oven to 325°F. Line two 12-well muffin tins with paper liners. Place the butter and sugar in the work bowl of a stand mixer fitted with the paddle attachment and cream until it is pale and fluffy, about 5 minutes.

2. Incorporate the eggs one at a time, scraping down the work bowl as needed. Add the sour cream and beat to incorporate. Scrape down the work bowl, gradually add the remaining ingredients, and beat until the mixture just comes together as a smooth batter.

3. Pour the batter into the paper liners, place the muffins in the oven, and bake until they are golden brown and a knife inserted into their centers comes out clean, 15 to 20 minutes.

4. Remove the muffins from the oven and let them cool before enjoying.

THE KERNELS OF SOUTHERN CUISINE

BY ALEXANDER LOPEZ-WILSON

The production of corn has been tied to the history of Southern cuisine since the beginning of the United States. During the colonial history of the Americas, the holdings of the Carolinas and Georgia grew various styles of corn to suit the various terrains of the region. In the granitic soils of the Appalachians, small-grained flint corn was adopted from the native Cherokee. In these regions, farming was mainly on a subsistence basis, with poor white farmers relying on corn production as their key source of vegetables, creating staples such as grits. Fodder from corn provided the main source of food for the protein for the population, pigs. In the 1850s, Georgians alone were consuming 2.2 million pigs a year.

The plantation farmers of the Atlantic Coast focused on production of cash crops such as indigo, tobacco, cotton, and rice. Production of these exported crops was facilitated by the mass enslavement of Africans. To feed the enslaved persons whose labor provided for their wealth, the slave-owning aristocracy replicated the diet that they saw providing sustenance for lower classes of white farmers. For the enslaved populations in the South, corn was often the only food source provided by their exploiters. Corn fritters, cornbread, pone, and spoonbread are examples of the ways that corn came to be utilized by the slave population.

Around the time of American Independence, whiskey was made from rye and other grains. As Southern farmers sought to produce their own spirits, they used their own major food source. Unaged corn whiskey became a consistent tipple for subsistence farmers, and introducing barrel aging produced the whiskey that would eventually become known as bourbon.

This corny tradition of Southern cuisine and drink remains intact to this day. Traveling the food cultures of the South, from the coastal shrimp and grits and the barbecue that still relies on corn-fed pork, to bourbon, corn and the South have proven to be inseparable.

APPETIZERS & SNACKS

Call them appetizers, hors d'oeuvres, bites, small plates, snacks, tapas, or charcuterie, this format is how one most often encounters a food-and-drink pairing. This is even the case in an informal setting: food prepared in this style is commonplace at the whiskey events I've attended, and that food is carefully selected to match the whiskey on offer. The virtue of bite-sized or small dishes is that they allow one to easily put together an ensemble featuring different flavors, and thus present a diverse selection of whiskeys to go with it, all without the workload or belly-filling qualities of a multicourse meal. This format is ideal for parties, events that call for standing and mingling, or a tasting that wants whiskey to be center stage.

YIELD: **4 TO 6 SERVINGS**

ACTIVE TIME: **15 MINUTES**

TOTAL TIME: **15 MINUTES**

COURTESY OF PAINTED STAVE DISTILLING

AVOCADO TOAST

With the avocado, queso fresco, and corn nibblets, this fancy toast has a luscious, corn-forward character. Best to reach for the corn whiskey, and Painted Stave's Bottled in Bond Corn Whiskey is one of the few properly aged choices in the category.

¼ cup canned corn, drained

4 to 6 slices of Sourdough Bread (see page 236)

Flesh from 2 avocados, mashed

Crema or sour cream, to taste

Fresh cilantro, chopped, for garnish

1. Warm a large cast-iron skillet over medium heat. Place the corn in the dry skillet and cook, stirring occasionally, until the corn is lightly charred, 6 to 10 minutes. Remove the pan from heat.

2. Place the slices of bread in a toaster and toast them until golden brown.

3. Spread the mashed avocado over the slices of toasted bread. Top each slice with a dollop of crema and the charred corn, and garnish with cilantro.

YIELD: **12 SERVINGS**

ACTIVE TIME: **30 MINUTES**

TOTAL TIME: **1 HOUR AND 45 MINUTES**

BOURBON SHEPHERD'S PIE BITES

This refined take on the beloved comfort food is sure to be a hit at any gathering.

3 lbs. red potatoes

½ lb. cheddar cheese, shredded

2 tablespoons unsalted butter

1 small white onion, diced

1 carrot, peeled and diced

1 garlic clove, crushed

1 lb. ground beef

Salt and pepper, to taste

3 oz. Garrison Brothers Small Batch Bourbon

¼ cup peas

Fresh chives, finely chopped, for garnish

1. Preheat the oven to 375°F. Place the potatoes in the oven and bake until they are fork-tender, about 1 hour. Remove the potatoes from the oven and let them cool.

2. When the potatoes are cool enough to handle, cut them in half lengthwise and scoop the flesh into a bowl, making sure to leave a ½-inch-thick wall around the edge of each half. Set the hollowed-out halves aside. Add the cheese to the potatoes in the bowl and mash until the mixture is smooth.

3. Warm a large skillet over medium heat. Add the butter and melt it. Add the onion, carrot, and garlic and cook, stirring continually, for 2 minutes.

4. Add the ground beef, season it with salt and pepper, and cook until it is browned and cooked through, 6 to 8 minutes, breaking the beef up with a wooden spoon as it cooks.

5. Deglaze the pan with the bourbon, scraping up any browned bits from the bottom. Bring the mixture to a simmer, stir in the peas, and cook, stirring occasionally, until the peas are cooked through, 3 to 4 minutes. Remove the pan from heat.

6. Fill the hollowed-out potato halves with the ground beef mixture. Top with the cheesy mashed potatoes, garnish with chives, and serve.

YIELD: **6 SERVINGS**
ACTIVE TIME: **10 MINUTES**
TOTAL TIME: **40 MINUTES**

CHILI & LIME SHRIMP

Pair with Compass Box The Spice Tree Scotch Whisky, as this innovative blend has the zing needed to hang with this appetizer.

2 limes

6½ oz. brown sugar

1½ oz. Scotch whisky

24 large shrimp, shells removed, deveined

2 tablespoons canola oil

1 red chile pepper, stem and seeds removed, minced

1. Preheat the oven to 400°F. Grate one of the limes to remove the zest and set the lime zest aside. Squeeze the juice from the limes into a small saucepan, stir in the brown sugar and whisky, and warm the mixture over medium heat, stirring to dissolve the sugar. When the sugar has dissolved, raise the heat to high and bring the glaze to a boil. When the mixture has reduced, remove the pan from heat and stir in the lime zest. Set the glaze aside.

2. Place the shrimp in a baking dish in a single layer. Drizzle the canola oil over the shrimp and toss to coat. Brush the shrimp with the glaze and then sprinkle the chile pepper over them.

3. Place the shrimp in the oven and bake until they are cooked through and opaque, 10 to 15 minutes.

4. Remove the shrimp from the oven and let them cool slightly before serving.

YIELD: **8 SERVINGS**
ACTIVE TIME: **20 MINUTES**
TOTAL TIME: **20 MINUTES**

COURTESY OF GARRISON BROTHERS DISTILLERY

CHIPOTLE & BOURBON QUESO

The smoky and spicy elements of the chipotles bring out the best in this bold Texas bourbon.

¼ cup Garrison Brothers Small Batch Bourbon

1½ tablespoons cornstarch

1 cup milk

2 cups shredded cheddar cheese

2 tablespoons pureed chipotles in adobo

1 tablespoon chopped fresh cilantro

Tortilla chips, for serving

1. Place the bourbon and cornstarch in a small bowl and whisk to combine. Set the mixture aside.

2. Place the milk in a large saucepan and bring it to a simmer over medium heat. Gradually add the cheddar cheese, whisking until the cheese has melted and the mixture is smooth.

3. Stir in the bourbon mixture and the pureed chipotles. Cook, whisking continually, until the mixture has thickened slightly, 1 to 2 minutes.

4. Transfer the queso dip to a serving bowl, top it with the cilantro, and serve with tortilla chips.

YIELD: **6 SERVINGS**

ACTIVE TIME: **25 MINUTES**

TOTAL TIME: **40 MINUTES**

COURTESY OF GARRISON BROTHERS DISTILLERY

BOURBON SMOKIES

Ask yourself: Have pigs in a blanket ever failed to put a smile on people's faces?

¼ cup Garrison Brothers bourbon

½ cup barbecue sauce

¼ cup water

½ lb. Hillshire Farm Lit'l Smokies sausages

2 (8 oz.) cans of Pillsbury Crescents dough

1. Preheat the oven to 375°F. Place the bourbon, barbecue sauce, water, and sausages in a saucepan and warm over medium heat. Cook, stirring occasionally, until the sausages are glazed and the liquid has reduced by half.

2. Strain the sausages, reserving the liquid as a dipping sauce. Place the sausages on a baking sheet and let them cool completely.

3. Separate the dough into triangles. Cut each triangle evenly into three strips.

4. Line a baking sheet with parchment paper. Wrap each sausage in a strip of dough and place them on the parchment-lined baking sheet. Place the wrapped sausages in the oven and bake until the dough is cooked through and golden brown, about 5 minutes.

5. Serve the bourbon smokies alongside the dipping sauces.

COURTESY OF PAINTED STAVE DISTILLING

GOAT CHEESE, DATE & PISTACHIO FOCACCIA

Pair this elevated toast with Painted Stave Bottled in Bond Bourbon. Painted Stave uses a high-rye mash for their bourbon, giving it an extra spicy, dry kick that provides a nice contrast here.

1 Focaccia (see page 240)

1 cup whipped goat cheese

¼ cup chopped dates

¼ cup pistachios, chopped

Pomegranate molasses, to taste

1. Preheat the oven to 375°F. Cut the Focaccia into squares, place them on a baking sheet, and place them in the oven. Toast until golden brown, 6 to 8 minutes.

2. Remove the toasted focaccia from the oven, spread the goat cheese over the top, and sprinkle the dates and pistachios over the goat cheese. Drizzle pomegranate molasses over the pieces of toasted focaccia and enjoy.

PAINTED STAVE DISTILLING

Located in Smyrna, Delaware, Painted Stave is focused on blending fundamentals of traditional distilling and modern technology to produce exemplary, innovative spirits. Their reliance on only the best local ingredients keeps the runs of those spirits in small batches, but Painted Stave has more than enough on offer. In addition to vodka and gin, Painted Stave produces five different types of whiskey. This entire fleet of whiskeys is remarkable, with the best of the bunch being the Diamond State Pot Still Whiskey, which more than nods to the whiskeys of the Ireland, and the bottled in bond rye. Keep an eye on them in the years to come.

SESAME WINGS

Pair with Michter's US*1 Sour Mash Whiskey. Michter's Sour Mash Whiskey doesn't get its name from using the sour mash process, but because it's made in such a way as to not quite be a bourbon or a rye. It complements not just the main elements in these sesame wings, but the specific balance of those flavors.

½ cup packed light brown sugar

3 tablespoons fresh lemon juice

3 garlic cloves, smashed

2-inch piece of fresh ginger, peeled and grated

1 teaspoon salt, plus more to taste

1 tablespoon sriracha, plus more for serving

1 tablespoon sesame seeds, toasted, plus more for garnish

3 lbs. chicken wings

Scallions, sliced thin, for garnish

Fresh cilantro, chopped, for garnish

1. Preheat the oven to 475°F. Place the brown sugar, lemon juice, garlic, ginger, and the salt in a saucepan and stir to combine. Bring the mixture to a boil, reduce the heat so that everything simmers, and cook, stirring occasionally, until the mixture is syrupy, about 20 minutes.

2. Strain the glaze through a fine mesh sieve (you should have about ⅔ cup). Stir in the sriracha and toasted sesame seeds.

3. While the glaze is simmering, place the chicken wings in an even layer on a rimmed baking sheet and season them with salt. Place the chicken wings in the oven and bake until they are lightly golden brown, 20 to 25 minutes.

4. Remove the chicken wings from the oven and place them in a large bowl. Add half of the sauce and toss until the chicken wings are coated.

5. Place the chicken wings back on the baking sheet and return them to the oven. Bake until the glaze has caramelized, 5 to 7 minutes.

6. Remove the chicken wings from the oven, garnish with additional sesame seeds, scallions, and cilantro, and serve with the remaining sauce and additional sriracha.

YIELD: **12 SERVINGS**

ACTIVE TIME: **25 MINUTES**

TOTAL TIME: **1 HOUR AND 15 MINUTES**

WHISKY-CURED SALMON

This recipe intends to replicate the flavor of smoked salmon. No cooking is required, just a little preparation the day before. If you do use smoked salmon, the Scotch will only further enhance that characteristic.

1 lb. smoked or unsmoked salmon, deboned, skin removed, and sliced

Salt, as needed

Sugar, as needed

Black Bottle or Finlaggan Old Reserve Scotch Whisky

1. Place the salmon on a sheet of plastic wrap, leaving wide borders around the top, bottom, and sides of the plastic wrap.

2. Sprinkle salt and sugar over the salmon until the surface is lightly coated. Drizzle a light coating of the whisky over the salmon, fold the plastic wrap over the salmon, and place it on a large plate or in a baking dish. Place the salmon in the refrigerator and let it cure for 12 hours before enjoying.

ON BOARD

A good charcuterie board provides a culinary kaleidoscope: cured meats, cheese, pickles, berries, nuts, crackers, and whatever else can be made to fit the theme. However many elements are put on the board, the stars are the cured meats and cheeses. This is a good thing in terms of potential whiskey pairings, as items in each of these categories are fatty and substantial enough to stand up well next to a Glencairn of whiskey. With all the different kinds of foods that can be organized into a charcuterie platter, my advice is to pick your four lead elements on the board and use them as the guide for constructing a flight of whiskeys. Some suggestions for pairings:

CHEESE

- Aged cheddar and **Dad's Hat Bottled in Bond Rye Whiskey**

- Aged gouda and **New Riff Straight Bourbon**

- Brie and **The Glenmorangie 10 Year Old Single Malt**

- Camembert and **James E. Pepper Rye Whiskey**

- Comte and **Skapa Skiren Single Malt**

- Dubliner and **Jameson Black Barrel**

- Gorgonzola and **Glendronach Allardice**

- Langres and **Four Roses Small Batch Select Bourbon**

- Mild cheddar and **Teeling Small Batch Irish Whiskey**

- Stilton and **Highland Park 12 Year Old**

- Roquefort and **Talisker 10 Year Old Single Malt**

CURED MEATS

- Bresaola and Old Pulteney 12 Year Old Single Malt

- Chorizo and Four Roses Small Batch Bourbon

- Cured venison and Aberlour A'Bunadh Single Malt or Glenfarclas 105 Single Malt

- Pâté de fois gras with Glenmorangie Nectar D'Or 12 Year Old Single Malt

- Pâté en terrine with Angel's Envy Bourbon

- Prosciutto and The Glenlivet 12 Year Old Single Malt

- Salami and Basil Hayden Bourbon

NUTS & OTHER POPULAR NOSH

- Smoked almonds and George Dickel No. 12 Tennessee Whiskey

- Roasted cashews and Ardbeg 10 Year Old Single Malt

- Sour pickles with Stranahan's American Single Malt

- Tinned sardines and Lagavulin 16 Year Old Single Malt

YIELD: **8 SERVINGS**

ACTIVE TIME: **3 HOURS**

TOTAL TIME: **4 HOURS**

COURTESY OF CHEF JORDAN WHITNEY

BOILED PEANUT HUMMUS

If you have some extra rub from the Pork Belly Burnt Ends, you also have the beginnings of this barbecue-style appetizer. As this hummus is not just nutty, but also earthy, Woodford Reserve Master's Collection Batch Proof Bourbon is a good match.

3 cups raw peanuts, in their shells

1 cup spice rub from Pork Belly Burnt Ends (see page 160)

1 to 2 tablespoons tahini paste

Juice of 1 lemon

1 tablespoon extra-virgin olive oil

Salt and pepper, to taste

Crudités, for serving

Pita chips, for serving

1. Place the raw peanuts and spice rub in a large saucepan and cover with water. Bring to a boil, reduce the heat so that the peanuts simmer, and cook, stirring occasionally, until the peanuts are soft enough to squish between two fingers, 2 to 3 hours. Add water as necessary to keep the peanuts covered.

2. Drain the peanuts, reserving the cooking liquid, and let the peanuts and liquid cool.

3. Place the peanuts in a food processor with 1 or 2 tablespoons of tahini, a squeeze of lemon juice, the olive oil, and ½ cup of reserved cooking liquid. Blitz until the mixture is smooth. Taste, season the hummus with salt and pepper, and taste again. Adjust the seasoning as necessary and enjoy with crudités and pita chips.

YIELD: **4 TO 6 SERVINGS**

ACTIVE TIME: **30 MINUTES**

TOTAL TIME: **3 HOURS AND 30 MINUTES**

COURTESY OF PAINTED STAVE DISTILLING

SHORT RIB & RYE TOAST

Pair with Painted Stave Bottled in Bond Rye Whiskey. It's more than just the rye bread that cries out for rye whiskey as a complement. The short rib topping calls for something especially robust, and Painted Stave's Maryland-style rye (mash bill of 70% rye, 25% corn, 5% malted barley) meets that requirement.

1 lb. beef short ribs

Salt and pepper, to taste

2 tablespoons canola oil

1 small yellow onion, chopped

1 carrot, peeled and chopped

1 celery stalk, chopped

2 garlic cloves, crushed

1 teaspoon dried thyme

½ cup red wine

2 cups Beef Stock (see page 246)

4 to 6 slices of marble rye bread

Horseradish Cream (see page 249), for serving

1. Season the short ribs with salt and pepper and let them sit at room temperature for 1 hour.

2. Place the canola oil in a Dutch oven and warm it over medium-high heat. Add the short ribs to the pot and sear until they are browned all over, turning them as they cook. Remove the short ribs from the pot and set them aside.

3. Add the onion, carrot, celery, garlic, and thyme to the pot and cook, stirring frequently, until the vegetables have softened and are starting to caramelize, about 8 minutes.

4. Deglaze the pot with the red wine, scraping up any browned bits from the bottom. Return the short ribs to the pot and add the stock. Reduce the heat to medium-low, cover the Dutch oven, and braise the ribs until they are so tender that they start to fall apart, about 2½ hours.

5. Remove the short ribs from the pot and shred the meat with a fork. Place the bread in a toaster and toast until golden brown.

6. Top the slices of toasted bread with the short ribs. Top each portion with some of the Horseradish Cream and enjoy..

COURTESY OF CHEF TRAVIS CLIFFORD,
San Diego, California

CARAMELIZED SPRING ONION DIP

"Spring onions are one of my favorite treats at the farmers market here in San Diego. Earthy sweet with a grassy bite, they are also regularly available at the world-famous Chino Farms in Rancho Santa Fe, California. Combined with sour cream and Greek yogurt, they make for a fantastic dip that is sure to please the masses," Clifford says. He enthusiastically recommends the E. H. Taylor Straight Rye for a pairing, saying, "I get a cracker-dry, sourdough-funk from the E. H. Taylor Straight Rye, and it has the bright, spicy backbone to hold up well with the fatty, earthy, and sweet dip."

3 lbs. spring onions, rinsed well and patted dry

2 tablespoons unsalted butter

2 cups mayonnaise

1 cup sour cream

1 cup plain full-fat Greek yogurt

Zest and juice of 2 lemons

1 teaspoon kosher salt

½ teaspoon black pepper

¼ teaspoon onion powder

¼ teaspoon garlic powder

Pita or Sourdough Bread (see page 237 or 236), toasted, for serving

1. Slice the spring onions thin from the top of the green part to the bottom of the white bulb. Place the butter in a large skillet and melt it over medium heat. Add the spring onions and reduce the heat to low. Cook the spring onions, stirring every few minutes, until they are golden brown, 10 to 12 minutes.

2. Remove the onions from the pan, place them in a large mixing bowl, and chill them in the refrigerator until completely cool.

3. Remove the spring onions from the refrigerator, add the remaining ingredients to the bowl, and stir to combine. Cover the bowl with plastic wrap and chill the dip in the refrigerator for at least 1 hour. If time allows, chill the dip in the refrigerator overnight. Serve with toasted pita or sourdough.

CALIFORNIA: CULTURE AND CUISINE COMING TOGETHER

BY SARAH JELTEMA

My home, San Diego, has roots in many different cultures. The best chefs in this region push boundaries and take massive risks, a boldness fostered by access to an abundance of fresh and local ingredients. Combine these two factors, and the result is inventive recipes that inspire and delight.

This fortunate clash is representative of California as a whole. The state is known for being home to the freshest produce in the United States. Over a third of the country's vegetables and two-thirds of its fruits and nuts are grown in the Golden State. On top of that, the sprawling coastline provides easy access to fresh seafood, from Dungeness crab to swordfish. Having this bounty available immediately allows restaurants to buy the exact amounts they need, keeping costs down and allowing chefs to get creative. The result is gastronomy that is not just "fusion," not just "local," but a rich combination of traditional cultures taking risks with their cuisine.

California's rich diversity extends into the culinary world. Nearly one in three restaurant workers in the area immigrated to the United States. This melting pot drives considerable change in the industry. Just think about it—if someone is willing to sacrifice it all to start over in a new country, taking risks in their cooking and exploring new areas is nothing.

In San Diego, creativity extends into more than just food—craft whiskey is starting to rise. The West Coast has always been known for lighter drinks like beer and wine, and California still has the most microbreweries of any state. As a result, most California whiskey distillers have a brewing or brandy background, a reality that has resulted in innovative whiskies that experiment with wine finishing, locally toasted malts, and even hops.

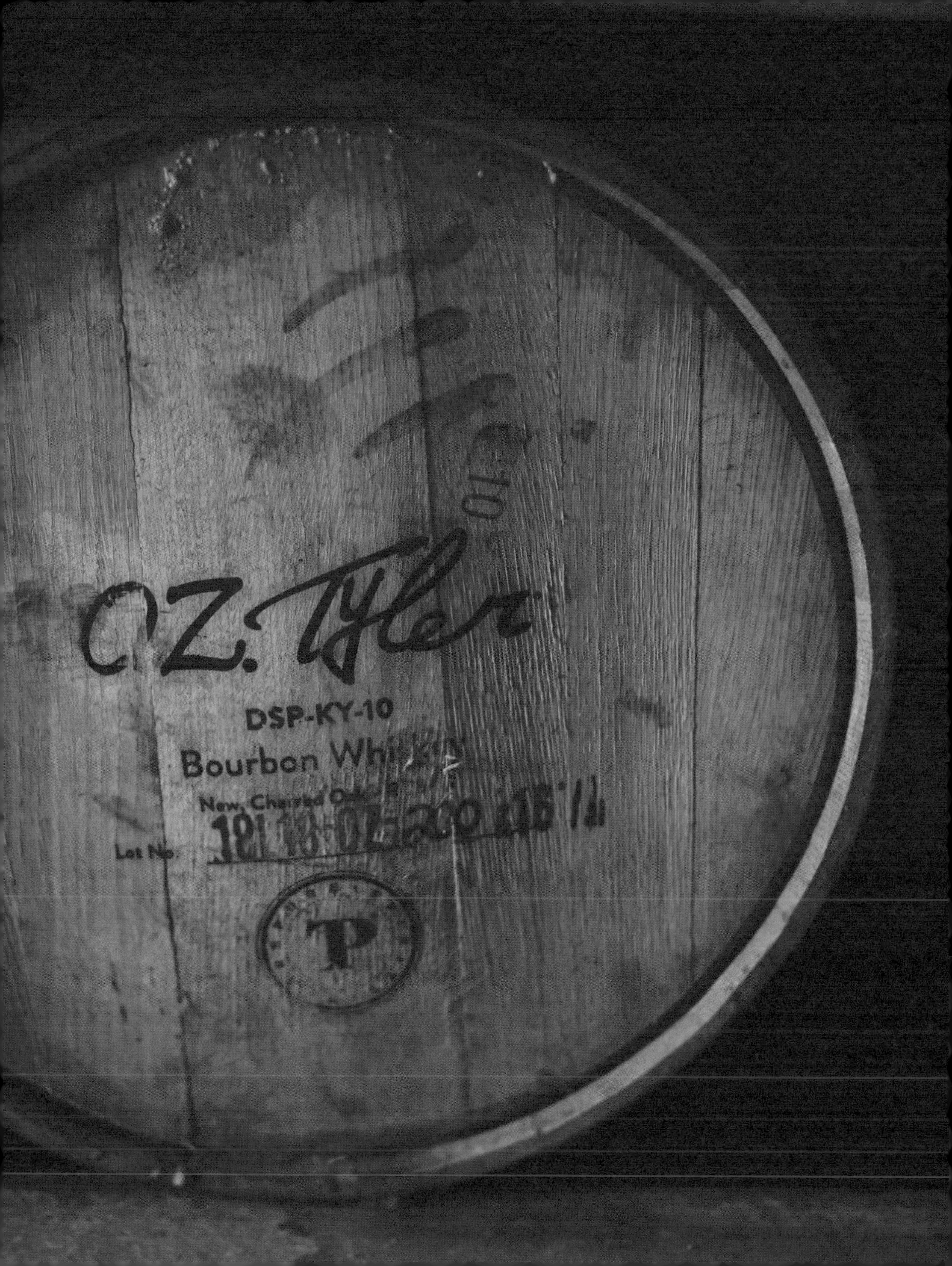
O.Z. Tyler
DSP-KY-10
Bourbon
Lot No.

YIELD: **4 TO 6 SERVINGS**

ACTIVE TIME: **40 MINUTES**

TOTAL TIME: **1 HOUR AND 15 MINUTES**

COURTESY OF CHEF CARLIE CORNETT
of True North Catering, Louisville, Kentucky

BACON-WRAPPED SHRIMP
WITH BLACKBERRY BOURBON BARBECUE SAUCE

Four Roses' subtle sweetness is a wonderful counter to the tart blackberries.

For the Sauce

2 cups ketchup

2 cups blackberries

1 cup Four Roses Small Batch Bourbon

6 tablespoons brown sugar

6 tablespoons light molasses

6 tablespoons apple cider vinegar

¼ cup Worcestershire sauce

2 tablespoons soy sauce

2 tablespoons Dijon mustard

3 tablespoons liquid smoke

2 teaspoons onion powder

2 teaspoons minced garlic

1 teaspoon red pepper flakes

1 teaspoon black pepper

For the Shrimp

8 strips of bacon, halved crosswise

16 large shrimp, shells removed other than tails, deveined

1. To prepare the sauce, place all of the ingredients in a medium saucepan and bring to a boil over medium heat, stirring occasionally. Reduce the heat and simmer the sauce until it has reduced to about 4 cups and the flavor has developed to your liking, about 10 minutes, stirring frequently. Remove the pan from heat and let the sauce cool. When the sauce has cooled, place it in a food processor and puree until smooth. Store the sauce in the refrigerator.

2. To begin preparations for the shrimp, preheat the oven to 425°F. Place an oven-safe wire rack in a rimmed baking sheet. Place the bacon on the rack and cook the bacon until it is just about to become crispy, 5 to 10 minutes, depending on the thickness of the bacon. Remove the bacon from the oven and let it drain on a paper towel–lined plate.

3. When the bacon is cool enough to handle, wrap one piece around each shrimp, securing the bacon with a toothpick. Place the bacon-wrapped shrimp on the wire rack set in the baking sheet and place them in the oven.

4. Bake the shrimp until they are cooked through and the bacon is crispy, about 10 minutes. Remove the shrimp from the oven and serve alongside the barbecue sauce.

BRENT ELLIOTT TALKS BBQ

Master distiller Brent Elliott is a huge part of Four Roses' renaissance, having used his unique abilities to produce what many, including *Whisky Magazine*, believe to be the best Kentucky bourbon available at present. Elliott, who grew up in the western part of the Bluegrass State, is also a big fan of barbecue, a passion that has no doubt influenced the choices he makes while producing whiskey, as he discusses below.

"Having grown up in Owensboro, my original conception of barbecue was defined by the Western Kentucky style. I was probably in my teens before I realized this barbecue, though well recognized, was not as universally known as some other regional styles. Western Kentucky barbecue is still my favorite, and as I have come to appreciate and love the barbecue available in other regions, I now realize how unique my hometown barbecue is.

The Western Kentucky style of barbecue accentuates the rich flavors of the meat with tangy sauces that are considerably less sweet than those featured in most other styles. The dark, spicy flavors from its robust sauces and the smoked flavors of the meats need something structured, yet subtle for effective pairing.

The mellow and slightly sweet flavors of Four Roses Bourbon do more than pair with the strong and zesty flavors of the barbecue—they complement and create balance for a unique, interesting, and delicious combination. The bright and nuanced flavors in the barbecue and the bourbon find different spaces on the palate, and when they come together, the result is fantastic."

YIELD: **2 SERVINGS**

ACTIVE TIME: **30 MINUTES**

TOTAL TIME: **30 MINUTES**

COURTESY OF CHEF THEODORE SMITH,
The Lion's Share, San Diego, California

BISON & YELLOWTAIL TARTARE
WITH SMOKED TROUT ROE AND YUZU KOSHO VINAIGRETTE

Pair with Nikka Pure Malt or the Nikka Highball (see opposite page). The yuzu kosho calls for Japanese whisky, and the Nikka Pure Malt is an accessible bottle that still manages to mirror the complexity of this dish.

For the Vinaigrette

6 tablespoons extra-virgin olive oil

2 garlic cloves, minced

1 tablespoon yuzu kosho

2 tablespoons fresh yuzu juice

For the Tartare

4 oz. bison top round, trimmed to remove fat and silver skin, finely diced (¼-inch cubes)

4 oz. fresh yellowtail, bones, skin, and any bloodline removed, finely diced (¼-inch cubes)

½ oz. smoked trout roe

2 tablespoons yuzu kosho vinaigrette

Pinch of finely chopped fresh chives

Salt and pepper, to taste

Spicy aioli or mayonnaise, for garnish

Smoked paprika oil, for garnish

Potato chips, for serving

Crostini, for serving

1. To prepare the vinaigrette, place the olive oil in a skillet and warm it over medium heat. Add the garlic and cook, stirring continually, until it just starts to brown, about 1 minute. Remove the pan from heat and let it cool completely. Once the mixture is cool, whisk in the yuzu kosho and yuzu juice. Set the vinaigrette aside.

2. To prepare the tartare, place all of the ingredients, except those designated for garnish or serving, in a bowl and gently stir to combine, taking care not to crush the trout roe. Garnish with a spicy aioli or mayonnaise, or smoked paprika oil, and serve with potato chips or crostini.

YIELD: **1 DRINK**

ACTIVE TIME: **2 MINUTES**

TOTAL TIME: **2 MINUTES**

COURTESY OF CHEF THEODORE SMITH

NIKKA HIGHBALL

A long, refreshing cocktail with surprising complexity and depth.

1½ oz. Nikka Pure Malt 12 Year Old

¼ oz. Rhinehall Mango Brandy

⅛ oz. Vanilla Syrup (see page 254)

2 to 3 drops of 10% Citric Acid Solution (see page 256)

2 dashes of rosewater

3 oz. sparkling mineral water

1 strip of lemon peel, for garnish

1. Build the cocktail in a Highball glass filled with ice, adding the cocktail ingredients in the order listed.

2. Stir until chilled, express the strip of lemon peel over the cocktail, and then use it as a garnish.

NIKKA HIGHBALL, SEE PAGE 81

COURTESY OF JACKSON SKELTON,
Executive Chef at LouVino Restaurant & Wine
Bar, Louisville, Kentucky

HOT BROWN CROQUETTES
WITH BOURBON BACON JAM

The balance of sweet and spicy elements in New Riff's Bottled in Bond Bourbon, along with its full-bodied mouthfeel, go hand in glove with the bacon jam.

For the Roasted Tomatoes

1 lb. roma tomatoes, sliced thin

3 garlic cloves, minced

2 tablespoons chopped fresh oregano

1 teaspoon sugar

1 teaspoon kosher salt

For the Bourbon Bacon Jam

1 cup diced bacon

½ yellow onion, diced

4 garlic cloves, minced

1 cup packed brown sugar

½ cup sorghum

½ cup bourbon

1 teaspoon sriracha

1 teaspoon kosher salt

1 teaspoon fresh lemon juice

1 teaspoon soy sauce

1 teaspoon Worcestershire sauce

For the Hot Brown

½ cup extra-virgin olive oil, plus more as needed

¾ cup all-purpose flour, plus more as needed

1½ cups milk

½ cup Chicken Stock (see page 245)

½ cup minced bacon

½ cup finely diced smoked turkey

½ cup roasted tomatoes

1 cup chopped oyster mushrooms

½ teaspoon freshly grated nutmeg

Salt and pepper, to taste

2 large eggs

2 teaspoons water

1 cup bread crumbs

1. Preheat the oven to 350°F. To prepare the roasted tomatoes, place all of the ingredients in a baking dish and stir until combined. Place the dish in the oven and roast the tomatoes until they start to collapse, about 15 minutes. Remove the tomatoes from the oven and set them aside.

2. To prepare the bourbon bacon jam, place the bacon in small saucepan and cook it over medium heat, stirring occasionally, until it is crispy. Transfer the bacon to a paper towel–lined plate and drain most of the fat from the pan. Add the onion and garlic, reduce the heat to low, and cook, stirring frequently, until the onion is translucent, about 8 minutes. Return the bacon to the pan, add the remaining ingredients, and simmer until the mixture has thickened, about 10 minutes. Remove the jam from heat and let it cool.

3. To begin preparations for the hot brown, place the olive oil in a small saucepan and warm it over medium heat. Add the flour and cook, stirring continually, for 3 minutes. Add the milk in a slow stream, stirring continually.

4. When all of the milk has been incorporated, stir in the stock, reduce the heat to low, and cook, stirring frequently to prevent the mixture from burning, for 30 minutes.

5. Add the bacon, turkey, roasted tomatoes, oyster mushrooms, and nutmeg, season the hot brown with salt and pepper, and cook, stirring continually, for 2 to 3 minutes. Remove the pan from heat, taste, and adjust the seasoning as necessary.

6. Let the hot brown cool for 5 to 10 minutes. Coat a shallow baking dish with olive oil and place the hot brown in the dish. Refrigerate for at least 3 hours. If time allows, chill the hot brown overnight.

7. Dust a work surface with flour and carefully turn the hot brown onto it, gently tapping the baking dish if the hot brown is sticking. Cut the mixture into 1-inch cubes and, working with flour-dusted hands, roll the cubes into balls. Place the balls on a platter and chill in the refrigerator for 15 minutes.

8. Line a baking sheet with parchment paper. Add olive oil to a large, deep skillet until it is about ½ inch deep and warm it to 355°F. Place the eggs and the water in a wide bowl and beat until combined. Place the bread crumbs in a separate wide bowl. Dip the hot brown croquettes in the egg wash, shake to remove any excess, and then dredge them in the bread crumbs until completely coated.

9. Working in batches to avoid crowding the pan, gently slip the croquettes into the hot oil and fry them until golden brown all over, turning them as necessary. Transfer the fried croquettes to a paper towel–lined plate to drain.

10. To serve, smear a small amount of the jam on a serving plate. Arrange the croquettes on top and top with more of the jam.

NEW RIFF DISTILLING

An independent, family-owned distillery, New Riff opened a state-of-the-art facility in Newport, Kentucky, in 2014, and very quickly caught the eye of industry insiders and aficionados with their Bottled in Bond offering.

Consisting of a mash bill of 65% corn, 30% rye, and 5% malted barley, New Riff's first bourbon turned out to be very different from other high-rye products. Intense but smooth, its sweet side stays just ahead of thespice. It's like a spicy herbal tea with a few cubes of demerara and half a teaspoon of vanilla extract stirred in. The spice from the high-rye content kicks with full force at the finish, before eventually turning minty.

NEWPORT, KENTUCKY
NEW RIFF DISTILLING, LLC
FILL DATE: 8/12/14
Bourbon Whiskey
NEWPORT KENTUCKY
NEW RIFF DISTILLING

PAIRING WHISKEY WITH OYSTERS,
SEE PAGE 90

A PERFECT PAIR

Sometimes I think that whiskey was predestined to be paired with oysters, Scotch in particular. Those Scottish malts aged on islands and coastal areas complement raw oysters perfectly, so much so that a splash of Scotch is frequently poured right into the shell. Yet, if one chooses to go for contrast instead accompaniment, the sweeter American and Irish whiskeys are better suited to that tack.

PAIRING WITH RAW OYSTERS

Back in the day, one simply ordered a plate of oysters on the half-shell or picked up a bag from the marina and that was that. Whatever was on offer was what you got, and therefore the distinctions mattered less. Nowadays, the choices for raw oysters have multiplied. Those choices are based on regional varietals, and where an oyster was farmed within that region and when it was harvested can have quite a bit to do with size and flavor.

ATLANTIC: Don't listen to anyone who dismisses these as the "Budweiser of oysters," because the varietal has plenty of character. Atlantics are the oyster benchmark for size, saline, and mineral notes, so when an oyster is described as big and fleshy or ultra-briny, it is in relation to Altantics. Moreover, if you really want to come to grips with how different a given species of oyster can be based on what farm it was grown in, just order a mixed plate of New York Blue Points, Chesapeake Bay oysters, and Gulf oysters. All three are Atlantics, but side by side it might very well seem their only relation is in being molluscs.

Pair With: Oban 12 Year Old or Clynelish 14 Year Old, with their saltwater taffy notes, make good company for most Atlantic oysters. Another good choice is the sea air-meets-vanilla character found in Jefferson's Ocean bourbons.

BELON: Also known as European Flats, they are the bedrock of French oyster culture. If you are enjoying oysters on the Continent, most likely they will be either Belons or Pacifics (which are widely farmed there). Belons are, as you may have guessed, flat, and their flesh has a creamy texture. In terms of flavor, they are usually as briny as a typical Atlantic oyster, but much more minerally, giving them an almost metallic flavor.

Pair With: If you find yourself in Scotland or Ireland, by all means pair Belons with whatever single pot still or single malt is at hand; you can't go wrong putting Galway oysters and Dingle Single Malt together, for example. In France or Portugal, look for Old Pulteney Navigator, Rock Island, or Talisker 10 Year.

OLYMPIA: The native oyster of the Pacific Northwest is quite small but varies widely in shape. Some are round and some an elongated ovoid. They pack a lot of flavor into that small stature, however. Their mineral note is strong enough to be reminiscent of copper, while their sweet side reaches to parsnips.

Pair With: Bunnahabhain 12 Year Old or Kilchoman Sanaig.

KUMAMOTO (East Asian Pacific): Formerly lumped in with the Pacific varietals, Kumamotos have recently become distinguished as their own species. While small, not-salty, and sweet, they have a distinct nutty note that separates them from their Pacific cousins.

Pair With: Hibiki Harmony or The Glenkinchie 12 Year Old complement Kumamotos nicely.

PACIFIC: These are by far the most-farmed oysters in the world, and so are available just about everywhere. They are known for being small in size, low in salinity, and having a melon-like sweetness. They occasionally carry a grassy note as well.

Pair With: Skapa Skiren, Bowmore 12 Year Old, and Talisker Storm are all good company for Pacific oysters, each in their own way.

SYDNEY ROCK OYSTERS: These are often the smallest of dining oysters, with a large one rarely exceeding three inches long *in the shell*. As is so often the case with small oysters, they punch above their weight in terms of flavor. In my experience, Sydney Rocks are the most minerally oyster, though not so much that one can't enjoy the grassy note that comes with them.

Pair With: Longbank 15 Year Old, hands down.

DREDGE: These Southern Hemisphere oysters are also known as Chilean oysters or Bluff oysters. They are renowned for their clean, delicate flavor, with the expected creamy, briny, and minerally notes far more muted.

Pair with: Working with the subtle flavors of these oysters is a necessity, so reach for AnCnoc 12 Year or BenRiach 10 Year.

BROILED OYSTERS WITH WHISKY & SMOKED CHEESE, SEE PAGE 94

YIELD: **2 TO 4 SERVINGS**
ACTIVE TIME: **15 MINUTES**
TOTAL TIME: **25 MINUTES**

BROILED OYSTERS
WITH WHISKY & SMOKED CHEESE

A tip: to cook oysters in the oven, whether roasting, baking, or broiling, and ensure they all remain upright, pour a thick layer of kosher salt into the bottom of a pan, and nestle the oysters, face up, into the salt.

12 oysters, unshucked

4 tablespoons unsalted butter, softened

3 garlic cloves, crushed

½ teaspoon cayenne pepper, to taste

2 to 4 dashes of Worcestershire sauce

1½ oz. Ardbeg 10 Year Old Whisky

¼ cup chopped fresh parsley

¼ cup freshly grated smoked Parmesan cheese

¼ cup bread crumbs

1. Shuck the oysters, keeping them on the half-shell. Discard the empty shells.

2. Place the butter in a saucepan and melt it over medium heat. Add the garlic, cayenne, and Worcestershire sauce and cook, stirring continually, until the garlic is lightly browned, about 2 minutes.

3. Remove the pan from heat and stir in the whisky. Set the sauce aside.

4. In a separate bowl, combine the parsley, Parmesan, and bread crumbs.

5. Preheat the broiler on the oven and position a rack in the upper part of the oven. Place the oysters in a cast-iron skillet and top each one with a dollop of the butter sauce and some of the Parmesan mixture. Place the oysters beneath the broiler, leaving the door open so that you can watch them closely. Broil the oysters until they are golden brown and the liquid is bubbling, 3 to 5 minutes. Remove the oysters from the oven and enjoy.

YIELD: **2 TO 4 SERVINGS**

ACTIVE TIME: **15 MINUTES**

TOTAL TIME: **25 MINUTES**

OYSTERS ROCKEFELLER

For my part, I jump at any chance to pair oysters with an American whiskey. With its thick layer of spinach and cheese, Oysters Rockefeller is usually the dish that provides that chance. Four Roses Yellow Label, with its balanced flavor and silky mouthfeel, is a great choice here.

4 tablespoons unsalted butter

4 oz. spinach, torn

2 shallots, minced

Juice of ½ lemon

½ cup freshly grated Romano cheese

Salt and pepper, to taste

18 oysters, unshucked

1. Preheat the oven to 450°F. Place the butter in a large skillet and melt it over medium heat. Add the shallots and cook, stirring occasionally, until they are translucent, about 3 minutes. Stir in the spinach and cook until it has wilted, about 2 minutes.

2. Remove the pan from heat, stir in the lemon juice and Romano cheese, and season the mixture with pepper.

3. Shuck the oysters, keeping them on the half-shell. Season them with salt, unless they are especially briny, and top with some of the spinach mixture.

4. Place the oysters, face up, in a cast-iron skillet, place them in the oven, and bake for 6 to 8 minutes. Remove the oysters from the oven and enjoy.

GRILLED OYSTERS WITH BLUE CHEESE, SEE PAGE 98

YIELD: **2 TO 4 SERVINGS**

ACTIVE TIME: **15 MINUTES**

TOTAL TIME: **25 MINUTES**

GRILLED OYSTERS WITH BLUE CHEESE

Pair With Caol Ila 12 Year Old Scotch whisky. Caol Ila's malts are known for being rich while not overdoing the smoke, allowing its herbal and floral notes to sing. It complements this dish very well, especially if you grill over real charcoal and lend the oysters a little smoke of their own.

1 tablespoon unsalted butter

1 tablespoon chopped fresh tarragon

Salt and pepper, to taste

12 oysters, unshucked

½ cup crumbled blue cheese

1. Prepare a gas or charcoal grill for medium heat (about 400°F). Place the butter in a small skillet and cook it over medium heat until it starts to brown and giving off a nutty fragrance. Remove the pan from heat and stir in the tarragon, salt, and pepper. Set the browned butter aside.

2. Place the oysters on the grill and cook them until they open slightly. Remove the oysters from the grill and pry them open with a sturdy knife. Remove the top shell and place the oyster on the half-shell back on the grill, face-up. Top each oyster with a few drops of the browned butter and some of the blue cheese. Grill the oysters for another 5 minutes, remove them from the grill, and enjoy.

YIELD: **2 TO 4 SERVINGS**
ACTIVE TIME: **15 MINUTES**
TOTAL TIME: **25 MINUTES**

ROASTED GARLIC & CHILI OYSTERS

If you look at the ingredients here, you can see how the staple fruit, vanilla, and spice notes of a blended Irish Whiskey would work well. Teeling Small Batch Irish Whiskey takes that affinity one extra step further, matching the brown sugar element by finishing their Small Batch in rum casks for a month.

18 oysters, unshucked

¾ cup unsalted butter, softened

2 tablespoons brown sugar

1 teaspoon garlic powder

1 teaspoon chili powder

1. Preheat the oven to 400°F. Shuck the oysters, keeping them on the half-shell.

2. Place the butter, brown sugar, garlic powder, and chili powder in a bowl and stir until well combined.

3. Top each oyster with a spoonful of the seasoned butter, place them in a cast-iron skillet, face up, and place them in the oven. Bake the oysters, keeping a close eye on them, until the liquid has been bubbling for a minute or two and/ or the edges of the oysters are curling up, 4 to 6 minutes. Remove the oysters from the oven and enjoy.

YIELD: **4 SERVINGS**

ACTIVE TIME: **25 MINUTES**

TOTAL TIME: **1 HOUR**

COURTESY OF CHEF ADAM COOKE

CHICKEN & CHESTNUT SAUSAGES

If you like, you can also use ground turkey in these sausages. Pair with Nelson's Green Brier Tennessee Whiskey. The only current example of a wheated Tennessee whiskey, Nelson's provides the necessary nutty, spicy, and floral notes.

2 tablespoons extra-virgin olive oil

1 celery stalk, finely diced

1 white onion, finely diced

½ cup blanched chestnuts, finely diced

1 lb. ground chicken

2 slices of bacon, finely diced

1 cup heavy cream

Juice of 1 lemon

1 egg

Fresh sage, chopped, to taste

Freshly grated nutmeg, to taste

Fresh thyme, to taste

Salt and pepper, to taste

Sausage casings, rinsed well (optional)

1. Place 1 tablespoon of the olive oil in a medium skillet and warm it over medium heat. Add the celery, onion, and chestnuts and cook, stirring frequently, until they have softened, about 4 minutes, making sure that they do not brown. Transfer the mixture to a mixing bowl and let it cool.

2. When the vegetable-and-chestnut mixture has cooled slightly, add the chicken, bacon, cream, lemon juice, and egg and stir to combine. Season the mixture with sage, nutmeg, thyme, salt, and pepper and stir to incorporate. Place a small piece of the mixture in a skillet and cook it until browned. Taste and adjust the seasoning as desired.

3. Form the sausage into patties or stuff it into casings. To cook the sausage patties, place them in a skillet with the remaining olive oil and cook them until browned on both sides and cooked through, 8 to 10 minutes. To cook the sausage links, place them in a skillet and cook until well browned all over and cooked through, 15 to 18 minutes.

YIELD: **8 SERVINGS**

ACTIVE TIME: **40 MINUTES**

TOTAL TIME: **3 HOURS**

COURTESY OF CHEF ADAM COOKE

SMOKED TROUT CROQUETTES

Pair with Glenfiddich 12 Year Old Single Malt. It might seem a little odd to complement a Southern dish like this one with a Scottish single malt, but if you've ever been to Scotland, you know they are pretty big on trout, too.

1 lb. russet potatoes

¾ lb. smoked trout, flaked

Zest and juice of 1 lemon

1 garlic clove, grated

1 bunch of fresh chives, minced

Salt, to taste

Cayenne pepper, to taste

Canola oil, as needed

All-purpose flour, as needed

¼ cup mayonnaise

2 teaspoons Dijon mustard

1. Preheat the oven to 400°F. Line a baking sheet with parchment paper. Place the potatoes in the oven and bake until very tender, about 1 hour. Remove the potatoes from the oven, slice them in half, and let them cool.

2. Place the smoked trout in the work bowl of a stand mixer fitted with the paddle attachment. Add the lemon zest, garlic, and chives, season the mixture with salt and cayenne, and stir to combine. Remove the skin from the potatoes and press the flesh through a potato ricer and into the work bowl.

3. Beat the mixture until it is well combined and thick. Taste, adjust the seasoning as necessary, and form tablespoons of the mixture into balls. Place the balls on the parchment-lined baking sheet and chill them in the refrigerator for 1 hour.

4. Add canola oil to a Dutch oven until it is about 2 inches deep and warm it to 350°F. Place some flour in a shallow bowl. Remove the croquettes from the refrigerator and dredge them in the flour until lightly coated. Working in batches to avoid crowding the pot, gently slip the croquettes into the hot oil and fry them until golden brown, 3 to 4 minutes, turning them as necessary. Transfer the cooked croquettes to a paper towel–lined plate to drain.

5. Place the mayonnaise, mustard, and lemon juice in a small bowl and stir to combine. Serve this dipping sauce alongside the croquettes.

NELSON'S GREEN BRIER DISTILLERY

Located in Nashville, Tennessee, Nelson's Green Brier is the revival of what had been one of the biggest distilleries in the state prior to the enactment of statewide prohibition in 1909. It is very much a family business started by brothers Andy and Charles Nelson, descendants of the original owners. They entered their 2015 initial production run of wheated Tennessee Whiskey into 30-gallon barrels and released that as a sneak-peek release in 2017, but everything since that first run has gone into standard 53-gallon barrels. While the Nelsons waited on that stock of whiskey to mature, they relied upon the sourced whiskeys going into their Belle Meade brand, and finally released their own regular edition, white-labeled Nelson's Green Brier Tennessee Whiskey, in 2019.

SPANISH STYLINGS

BY EMMA BRIONES

If you think about Spain and food, the first thing that comes to most people's minds is tapas. If you ask for a drink at any bar in Spain, the response from the bartender will always be the same: "Do you want a snack to pair with it?" That's what a tapa is, a snack that has become something more.

Tapa means "cover" in Spanish, and this nickname for snacks comes from an ancient custom. They say that taverns and inns used to cover beer and wine glasses with a piece of bread or a slice of ham to prevent flies or dust from entering the glass. Also, Spaniards have a long tradition of snacking, which has turned the tapa into a lunch or dinner option. What began as bread, cheese, and/or ham evolved into pinchos (a combination of ingredients on a toothpick or on top of some bread). And, lately, into a smaller portion of what would typically be served as an entree.

When visiting Spain, you will find tapas everywhere. The possibilities are endless and this wide variety provides a range of options for whiskey pairings. And, while this might be unexpected for many, there is a great range of Spanish whiskies to pair them with.

Spanish whiskey isn't something new. In fact, it's been around since the early 1900s, though Spaniards never cared too much about it. But that has changed in the past decade, as some craft distillers found their calling and started producing remarkable whiskies. While we can't yet say that there's a definitive style for Spanish whiskey, it tends to carry attributes that work very well when paired with Spanish food.

As you might expect, there is a strong sherry influence in Spanish whiskey. The casks that hold this fortified wine from the south of Spain have been used to age whiskey around the world for a long time, and Spain, looking to utilize what is nearby, is part of this storied tradition. As there are a variety of sherries to bestow their flavor on a whiskey, it is easy to find a pairing for any tapa, whether it be something salty like croquetas or a rich offering such as beef shank coated with gravy.

YIELD: **8 SERVINGS**

ACTIVE TIME: **2 HOURS**

TOTAL TIME: **16 HOURS**

RECIPE COURTESY OF MARCOS SIERRA,
Executive Chef at the Intercontinental Hotel, Barcelona

PAIRING COURTESY OF WILLIAM GEOGHEGAN,
Food and Beverage Director at the Intercontinental

CHINESE BREAD TEQUEÑO

Pair with Drago 5 Year Old Whisky, a wheated Spanish product that carries the creamy, floral, and tropical notes we expect from vanilla. For more insight into what makes this pairing so exceptional, go to the sidebar on page 108.

4 large eggs

¾ cup plus ½ cup water

2 ⅔ oz. sugar

2 tablespoons honey

1 ⅔ cups all-purpose flour

1 teaspoon baking soda

½ teaspoon fine sea salt

Canola oil, as needed

7 oz. plantains, chopped

2 teaspoons cinnamon, plus more for dusting

1. Place the eggs, ¾ cup of water, the sugar, and honey in a mixing bowl and stir to combine. Gradually add the flour, baking soda, and salt and stir until the mixture comes together as a smooth dough. Form the dough into a ball, coat a bowl lightly with canola oil, and place the dough in it. Cover the bowl with plastic wrap and let it rest in the refrigerator overnight.

2. Place the plantains, remaining water, and cinnamon in a saucepan and simmer over medium-low heat until the plantains are tender, about 15 minutes. Remove the pan from heat and let the mixture cool for 1½ hours. After 1½ hours, mash the plantains, place them in a piping bag fitted with a fine tip, and set it aside.

3. Remove the dough from the refrigerator and cut it into 20 pieces. Form the pieces into seamless balls, place them on a piece of parchment paper, and let them rest for 30 minutes.

4. Add canola oil to a Dutch oven until it is about 2 inches deep and warm it to 375°F. Poke a hole into the balls of dough and pipe some of the mashed plantains into each one.

5. Working in batches to avoid crowding the pot, gently slip the balls of dough into the hot oil and cook until they are golden brown all over, turning them as necessary. Transfer the fried bread to a paper towel–lined plate and let them drain.

6. Dust the fried bread with cinnamon and enjoy.

TAPAS & TERROIR

BY EMMA BRIONES

Food is far more than the ingredients it consists of. It also shapes people's characters and helps them understand the world around them. Terroir is an important component in fostering this orientation. While sometimes you look for a pairing where the whiskey contrasts with the dish, you can also focus on the terroir, as the team at the Intercontinental Barcelona has done with gildas (see page 111), a traditional tapa from the north of Spain, with Bikkun Whisky, which is also produced in the region. This regional emphasis also guides the use of the clay pot, as it provides an earthy note that will keep the concept of terroir front of mind.

Terroir is also the idea behind the pairing the Chinese Bread Tequeño (see page 106) with Drago. Plantains are one of the biggest exports from the Canary Islands, where Drago's Single Grain is produced, with 100 percent of the wheat used in the whiskey produced on the island. This shared geography means the whiskey and tapa are fast friends. Even if one misses this connection, the vanilla notes of the whiskey and the cinnamon in the filling are so perfect a match that they can't be overlooked.

YIELD: **6 SERVINGS**

ACTIVE TIME: **10 MINUTES**

TOTAL TIME: **10 MINUTES**

RECIPE COURTESY OF MARCOS SIERRA
PAIRING COURTESY OF WILLIAM GEOGHEGAN

GILDAS IN THE OLIVE TREE

Pair with Bikkun Whisky or the Fumo cocktail (see page 112).

4 oz. anchovies in olive oil, drained and oil reserved

¼ cup water

¼ cup reserved oil from anchovies

2 cups Gordal olives, pits removed, marinated in olive oil and garlic

2 red chile peppers, stems and seeds removed, chopped

1. Place the anchovies, water, and olive oil in a food processor and puree until the mixture has emulsified.

2. Fill the olives with the anchovy puree, close each one up with a piece of chile pepper, and enjoy.

YIELD: **1 DRINK**

ACTIVE TIME: **2 MINUTES**

TOTAL TIME: **1 MONTH**

COURTESY OF ROGER RUEDA
AND GEORGE RESTREPO

FUMO

A Boulevardier take that resides at the highest levels of mixology.

1¼ oz. Bikkun Whiskey

1¼ oz. Dos Déus DIP Fumat (smoked vermouth)

1¼ oz. Campari Cask Tales

1. Combine all of the ingredients in a clay pot and let the mixture age for at least 1 month.

2. Pour the cocktail into a coupe or over ice in a rocks glass, garnish with an orange peel, and enjoy.

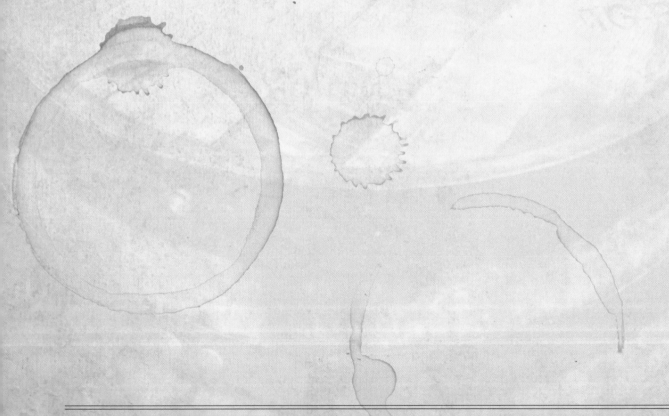

OCTOPUS WITH WHISKY, SEE PAGE 116

YIELD: **6 SERVINGS**

ACTIVE TIME: **30 MINUTES**

TOTAL TIME: **2 HOURS AND 30 MINUTES**

RECIPE COURTESY OF CHEF MARCOS SIERRA
PAIRINGS COURTESY OF WILLIAM GEOGHEGAN

OCTOPUS WITH WHISKY

To make this into a meal, serve it with a potato souffle. As a rule, if you are going to use whisky in a recipe, that is the whisky you pair with. Haran is produced in the Basque region, making it an appropriate partner for octopus, which is beloved in the area. Looking for something with a little more complexity? The Bacus (see opposite page) will work quite nicely.

3½ lb. octopus

Kosher salt, as needed

Sweet paprika, to taste

Pinch of Szechuan pepper

Pinch of allspice

Pinch of black pepper

Splash of Haran 18 Year Old Whisky

Extra-virgin olive oil, to taste

1. Preheat the oven to 350°F. Place the octopus in a baking dish, season it generously with salt, and let it rest for 30 minutes.

2. Rinse the octopus, pat it dry, and place it in a baking dish. Season the octopus with paprika, sprinkle the Szechuan pepper, allspice, and black pepper over it, and splash the whisky on top. Cover the baking dish with aluminum foil, place it in the oven, and braise the octopus until it is al dente, about 1½ hours.

3. Remove the octopus from the oven, cut off the tentacles, and chop them.

4. Place the pan juices in a small saucepan and reduce them over medium heat until the consistency is to your liking. Season the dressing with a bit of olive oil and salt, drizzle it over the octopus tentacles, and enjoy.

COURTESY OF ROGER RUEDA AND
GEORGE RESTREPO

BACUS

A sweet-and-tart cocktail that cuts beautifully against the fresh, briny flavor of the octopus.

2 oz. Haran 18 Year Old Whisky

⅔ oz. lime cordial

⅔ oz. blueberry cordial

⅔ oz. Vanilla Syrup (see page 254)

⅔ oz. water

Dash of black pepper

1. Place all of the ingredients in a mason jar and let the mixture age for at least 1 month.

2. Strain the cocktail into a tumbler and enjoy.

YIELD: **4 SERVINGS**

ACTIVE TIME: **15 MINUTES**

TOTAL TIME: **30 MINUTES**

RECIPE COURTESY OF CHEF MARCOS SIERRA
PAIRING COURTESY OF WILLIAM GEOGHEGAN

EGGPLANT WITH MISO

Pair with Sack Man 12 Year Old Whisky. Aged in sherry casks, it's easy to imagine how Sackman can supplement the delicately sweet Japanese eggplant.

Canola oil, as needed

1 long Japanese eggplant, halved lengthwise

10 tablespoons soy sauce

10 tablespoons red miso

10 tablespoons brown sugar

10 tablespoons Sack Man Bierbrand Whisky

Sesame seeds, for garnish

Fresh cilantro, chopped, for garnish

1. Add canola oil to a Dutch oven and heat it until it is about 350°F. Cut each half of eggplant into four pieces, gently slip them into the canola oil, and fry until golden brown and cooked through, 6 to 8 minutes, turning them as necessary. Transfer the fried eggplant to a paper towel–lined plate to drain.

2. Place the soy sauce, red miso, brown sugar, and whisky in a mixing bowl and whisk until combined.

3. Add the fried eggplant to the sauce and toss until coated. Garnish with the sesame seeds and cilantro and enjoy.

COURTESY OF EMMA BRIONES

TRADITIONAL CROQUETAS

Pair with Navazos Palazzi Single Palo Cortado Cask Whisky. Croquetas are a staple snack item in Spain, so it's fitting to make the whisky pairing as Spanish as possible, doubling down on the Spanish influence. Palo Cortado is a particularly rare version of sherry, adding its unique richness to the proceedings.

2 tablespoons extra-virgin olive oil, plus more as needed

1 onion, chopped

¼ cup all-purpose flour

¾ lb. finely diced leftover chicken, pork, or beef

3 cups milk

Pinch of freshly grated nutmeg

Salt, to taste

2 eggs, beaten

Bread crumbs, as needed

1. Place the olive oil in a medium skillet and warm it over medium heat. Add the onion and cook, stirring occasionally, until it starts to turn golden brown, about 6 minutes. Add the flour and cook, stirring continually, for 2 minutes.

2. Stir in the leftover meat and cook, stirring frequently, until it is warmed through, about 2 minutes. Add the milk in a slow stream, stirring until it is incorporated. Add the nutmeg, season the mixture with salt, and remove the pan from heat.

3. Cover a baking sheet with plastic wrap. Spread the mixture evenly over the baking sheet and cover it with a piece of parchment paper and more plastic wrap. Store the mixture in the refrigerator overnight.

4. Remove the baking sheet from the refrigerator. Add olive oil to a large, deep skillet until it is about 1 inch deep.

5. Place the beaten eggs in a bowl. Place bread crumbs in a separate bowl. Form the mixture into ovals, dredge them in the eggs, shake to remove excess, and dredge them in the bread crumbs until coated.

6. Working in batches to avoid crowding the pan, gently slip the croquetas into the hot oil and fry until golden brown, 4 to 5 minutes, turning them as necessary. Transfer the fried croquetas to a paper towel–lined plate to drain and season them with salt before serving.

SIDES, SAUCES & DRESSINGS

While the process of selecting the ideal whiskey to pair will receive the most attention when you're planning a menu, you can't lose sight of those elements that round out the table, and make for a truly great meal.

Featuring comforting classics that fit right in at a barbecue to elegant soups and sauces that will elevate a more-formal gathering, the preparations in this chapter will provide precisely what you need, complementing or contrasting the rest of your selections.

YIELD: **2 CUPS**

ACTIVE TIME: **15 MINUTES**

TOTAL TIME: **45 MINUTES**

BARBECUE SAUCE WITH SCOTCH

The standard is to reach for bourbon, Tennessee whiskey, or maybe rye when jazzing up a barbecue sauce. Scotch, however, can supply notes of smoke, wood, and honey, and play up those elements in a barbecue sauce just as easily as their American counterparts amplify the vanilla, maple, and spiciness.

2 tablespoons unsalted butter

2 large garlic cloves, diced

1 small yellow onion, diced

1 cup Tomato Sauce (see page 261)

⅓ cup brown sugar

1 tablespoon Worcestershire sauce

1 tablespoon white vinegar

3 oz. VAT 69, Famous Grouse, Johnnie Walker Black, or Black Bottle Scotch Whisky

1 tablespoon honey

2 teaspoons mustard powder

1 tablespoon chili powder

1 teaspoon kosher salt

1 teaspoon black pepper

1. Place the butter in a medium saucepan and melt it over medium heat. Add the garlic and onion and cook, stirring frequently, until the onion has softened, about 5 minutes.

2. Transfer the garlic and onion to a blender and puree until smooth. Place the puree in a clean saucepan, add the remaining ingredients, and stir until thoroughly combined.

3. Bring the sauce to a simmer over medium heat, cover the pan, and simmer the sauce until the flavor has developed to your liking, 20 to 30 minutes.

4. Remove the pan from heat and use the sauce as desired.

YIELD: **8 SERVINGS**

ACTIVE TIME: **30 MINUTES**

TOTAL TIME: **1 HOUR AND 15 MINUTES**

BACON MAC & CHEESE

For a heavy dish featuring cheese, pasta, and bacon, my first thought is bourbon, one that is full-bodied, drinkable neat, and has a clear note of barrel char running through it. To me, that means reach for the Knob Creek.

1 teaspoon kosher salt, plus more to taste

6 to 8 oz. macaroni

3 strips of thick-cut bacon

1 tablespoon unsalted butter

1 shallot, minced

2 garlic cloves, minced

1 tablespoon all-purpose flour

1 cup milk

½ lb. shredded cheddar cheese

4 oz. Parmesan cheese, freshly grated

¼ cup bread crumbs

1. Preheat the oven to 350°F. Bring water to a boil in a large saucepan. Add salt and the macaroni to the boiling water and cook until the macaroni is al dente, 6 to 8 minutes. Drain the macaroni, place it back in the saucepan, and set it aside.

2. While the water is coming to a boil in Step 1, place the bacon in a large skillet and cook until it is crispy and browned, 6 to 8 minutes, turning it as necessary. Transfer the cooked bacon to a paper towel–lined plate and let it drain. When the bacon is cool enough to handle, chop it into bite-size pieces.

3. Place the butter in a clean saucepan and melt it over medium heat. Add the shallot and garlic and cook, stirring frequently, until they have softened, about 5 minutes. Add the flour and salt and stir constantly until thoroughly incorporated.

4. While stirring continually, add the milk, half of the cheddar, and the Parmesan. Cook until the sauce is smooth and thick.

5. Add the sauce and chopped bacon to the macaroni and stir until combined. Transfer the mixture to a baking dish, smoothing the top so that it is even. Sprinkle the remaining cheddar over the top, top the cheese with the bread crumbs, and place the dish in the oven.

6. Bake until the top is golden brown and the mac & cheese is bubbling, 30 to 40 minutes. Remove the mac & cheese from the oven and let it cool slightly before serving.

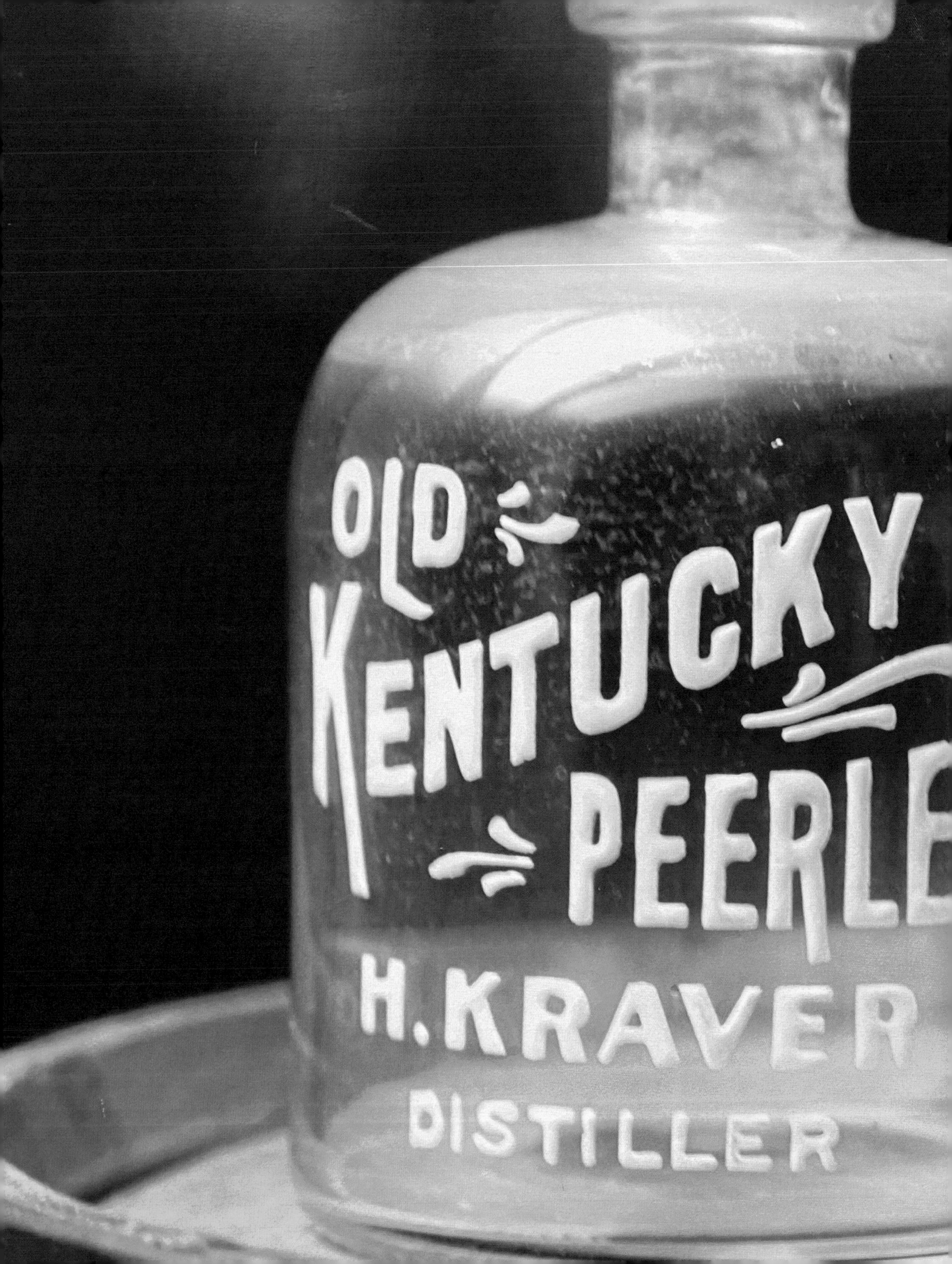
OLD
KENTUCKY
PEERLE
H. KRAVER
DISTILLER

DRINK
OLD KENTUCKY
EERLESS WHISKEY
H. KRAVER, Distiller
ENDERSON, - KENTUCKY

YIELD: **1 CUP**
ACTIVE TIME: **20 MINUTES**
TOTAL TIME: **30 MINUTES**

COURTESY OF MICHTER'S DISTILLERY

BROWN SUGAR BARBECUE SAUCE

Like all barbecue sauces, this can be used with most anything you want, but it is particularly good with chicken, pork chops, and pork ribs. What makes Michter's US*1 Bourbon the right choice here is its potent oaky notes, which complement the spicy kick. Additionally, its smoky depth enhances your grilling if you are doing so over charcoal—or supplies that element if you are taking the easy way out.

1 tablespoon extra-virgin olive oil

½ small yellow onion, minced

⅓ cup packed brown sugar

1 teaspoon kosher salt

½ teaspoon black pepper

⅔ cup ketchup

2 teaspoons Worcestershire sauce

¼ cup water

1. Place the olive oil in a medium saucepan and warm it over medium heat. Add the onion and cook, stirring occasionally, until it is translucent, about 3 minutes.

2. Add the remaining ingredients and stir to incorporate them. Bring the sauce to a boil, reduce the heat, and simmer until the sauce has thickened and the flavor has developed to your liking, 15 to 20 minutes. Use immediately or store in the refrigerator.

YIELD: **6 SERVINGS**
ACTIVE TIME: **20 MINUTES**
TOTAL TIME: **20 MINUTES**

COURTESY OF CHEF ADAM COOKE

PAN-ROASTED BRUSSELS SPROUTS
WITH PINE NUTS & PEARS

The sharp, peculiar flavor of Brussels sprouts would typically call for a rye whiskey, but this particular preparation has a sweet side. A Kentucky rye like Old Grand-Dad Bottled in Bond Bourbon is well suited to match that element.

¼ cup extra-virgin olive oil

1 sprig of fresh rosemary

1 lb. Brussels sprouts, trimmed and quartered

2 underripe green pears

1 small onion or shallot, sliced thin

1 cup pine nuts

½ cup balsamic vinegar

2 tablespoons unsalted butter

1 tablespoon honey

Parmesan cheese, shaved, for garnish

1. Warm a large skillet over high heat. Add the olive oil, warm it, and add the rosemary, Brussels sprouts, pears, onion, and pine nuts. Cook, without stirring, until the Brussels sprouts and pears are tender and browned, about 6 minutes.

2. Stir the mixture, add the balsamic vinegar, and toss to coat. Cook for 2 minutes, stir in the butter, and stir until everything is glazed.

3. Drizzle the honey over the dish, garnish with shaved Parmesan, and enjoy.

YIELD: **½ CUP**
ACTIVE TIME: **5 MINUTES**
TOTAL TIME: **5 MINUTES**

SWEET & SPICY HONEY GLAZE

Generously brush this glaze onto chicken, pork, seafood—particularly salmon and shrimp—and veggies while they are on the grill. One route to go for grilling accoutrements is the vinegar-driven path, and in such instances rye whiskey is a better accompaniment than bourbon. That goes double for Michter's US*1 Rye, which has a citrusy aspect that works particularly well here.

3 tablespoons honey

1 tablespoon whole-grain mustard

¼ cup water

2 tablespoons apple cider vinegar

Salt and pepper, to taste

1 teaspoon red pepper flakes

1. Place all of the ingredients in a mixing bowl and whisk until thoroughly combined.

SWEET & SPICY HONEY GLAZE,
SEE PAGE 133

YIELD: **2 CUPS**
ACTIVE TIME: **5 MINUTES**
TOTAL TIME: **5 MINUTES**

COURTESY OF CHEF BRETT DILLON FOR GARRISON BROTHERS DISTILLERY

BOURBON RANCH DRESSING

This is good as a dipping sauce or over a salad, and can also work nicely as a marinade.

¾ cup mayonnaise
¾ cup sour cream
¼ cup bourbon
1 tablespoon fresh lemon juice
1 tablespoon chopped fresh dill
1 tablespoon chopped fresh parsley
1 tablespoon chopped fresh oregano
Salt, to taste
1 tablespoon garlic powder
1 tablespoon onion powder

1. Place all of the ingredients in a mixing bowl and whisk until the dressing is smooth and well combined.

YIELD: **12 CUPS**

ACTIVE TIME: **30 MINUTES**

TOTAL TIME: **1 HOUR AND 30 MINUTES**

COURTESY OF CHEF REED JOHNSON,
Equus Restaurant, Louisville, Kentucky

KENTUCKY BOURBON & PEPPERCORN BARBECUE SAUCE

A lovely sauce to use on beef, particularly brisket.

¼ cup extra-virgin olive oil

6 garlic cloves, minced

1 lb. sweet Vidalia onions, diced

3 cups Weller Special Reserve Bourbon

1 lb. roasted red bell peppers, diced

1½ lbs. light brown sugar

1½ cups Worcestershire sauce

8 cups ketchup

4 cups apple cider vinegar

1 oz. coarsely ground black pepper

2 oz. kosher salt

2 tablespoons fresh lemon juice

1. Place the olive oil in a large stockpot and warm it over medium heat. Add the garlic and onions and cook, stirring frequently, until the onions are translucent, about 5 minutes.

2. Carefully stir two-thirds of the bourbon into the pot. Add the roasted peppers and brown sugar and cook, stirring until the brown sugar has dissolved.

3. Add the Worcestershire sauce, ketchup, and apple cider vinegar, stir until thoroughly incorporated, and simmer the sauce for 10 minutes.

4. Stir in the pepper, salt, and lemon juice, reduce the heat to low, and gently simmer the sauce until it has thickened and the flavor has developed to your liking, about 1 hour, stirring every 15 minutes.

5. Remove the pot from heat, stir in the remaining bourbon, and use the sauce as desired.

KENTUCKY BOURBON & PEPPERCORN
BARBECUE SAUCE, SEE PAGE 137

YIELD: **6 SERVINGS**

ACTIVE TIME: **15 MINUTES**

TOTAL TIME: **1 HOUR AND 45 MINUTES**

TENNESSEE MASHED SWEET POTATOES

Jack lends its legendary sweetness to this side, which will work well in any season.

1 lb. sweet potatoes

2 tablespoons extra-virgin olive oil

¼ cup brown sugar

1 tablespoon molasses

1 tablespoon unsalted butter

½ teaspoon cinnamon

¼ teaspoon freshly grated nutmeg

½ teaspoon pure vanilla extract

Salt, to taste

3 oz. Jack Daniel's Tennessee Whiskey

¼ cup heavy cream

1. Preheat the oven to 400°F. Rinse the sweet potatoes, pat them dry, and rub them with the olive oil. Place the sweet potatoes on a baking sheet, place them in the oven, and bake until they are tender enough that a knife inserted into their sides easily slides through to the center, about 1 hour. Remove the sweet potatoes from the oven and let them cool.

2. When the sweet potatoes are cool enough to handle, scoop the flesh into a mixing bowl. Add the brown sugar, molasses, butter, cinnamon, nutmeg, vanilla, and a pinch of salt and beat the mixture until it is smooth. Add the whiskey and heavy cream and beat until the mixture is smooth and creamy.

3. Place the mashed sweet potatoes in a saucepan, cook them over medium-low heat until warmed through, and enjoy.

CHEDDAR & SAGE BISCUITS,
SEE PAGE 144

YIELD: **12 BISCUITS**

ACTIVE TIME: **20 MINUTES**

TOTAL TIME: **1 HOUR**

COURTESY OF MICHTER'S DISTILLERY

CHEDDAR & SAGE BISCUITS

If you can find White Lilly flour, a popular Southern variety, these biscuits will become transcendent.

3¼ cups all-purpose flour, plus more as needed

2¼ teaspoons baking powder

½ teaspoon baking soda

1½ teaspoons kosher salt

1 cup unsalted butter, chilled and diced; plus 2 tablespoons, melted; plus more for serving

1 tablespoon chopped fresh sage

½ cup shredded white cheddar cheese

1 cup buttermilk, chilled

1½ oz. Michter's US*1 Rye Whiskey

½ teaspoon freshly ground black pepper

¼ teaspoon Maldon sea salt

Honey, for serving

1. Whisk the flour, baking powder, baking soda, and salt together in a large mixing bowl. Add the chilled butter and work the mixture with a pastry cutter until pea-sized clumps form. Add the sage, cheddar cheese, buttermilk, and rye and stir until the mixture just comes together as a dough.

2. Transfer the dough to a flour-dusted work surface and gently pat it into a rectangle that is about 1-inch thick. Use a bench scraper to cut the dough into 4 rectangles, and then carefully stack them on top of each other.

3. Line a baking sheet with parchment paper. Dust a rolling pin with flour and gently roll the stack into a 1-inch-thick square, keeping in mind that the shape isn't as important as the thickness. Using a flour-dusted mason jar or ring cutter, cut the dough into 12 biscuits, and place them on the baking sheet, leaving about 2 inches between each biscuit. Place the biscuits in the freezer for 10 to 15 minutes.

4. Preheat the oven to 425°F. Remove the biscuits from the freezer. Place the melted butter in a small bowl, stir to combine, and brush the tops of the biscuits. Sprinkle the pepper and salt over the biscuits, place them in the oven, and bake until the tops are golden brown, 15 to 20 minutes.

5. Remove the biscuits from the oven and serve with the honey and additional butter

YIELD: **6 TO 8 SERVINGS**

ACTIVE TIME: **20 MINUTES**

TOTAL TIME: **1 HOUR**

BOURBON BUTTERNUT SQUASH
WITH CRISPY SAGE & PARMESAN

Alongside the earthy sage, nutty Parmesan, sweet squash, the addition of Michter's bourbon makes this a very complex side dish.

2 large butternut squash, peeled and cut into 1-inch cubes

2 tablespoons extra-virgin olive oil

1 tablespoon kosher salt

1 tablespoon garlic powder

1 tablespoon onion powder

1½ teaspoons cinnamon

¼ teaspoon freshly ground black pepper

½ cup heavy cream

2 tablespoons Michter's US*1 Bourbon

4 tablespoons unsalted butter

¼ cup freshly grated Parmesan cheese, plus more for garnish

¼ cup canola oil

¼ cup fresh sage

1. Preheat the oven to 425°F. Line a baking sheet with aluminum foil. Place the butternut squash, olive oil, salt, garlic powder, onion powder, cinnamon, and black pepper in a large mixing bowl and toss to combine. Place the squash on the baking sheet, place it in the oven, and roast until it is fork-tender and browned, 30 to 35 minutes, stirring halfway through.

2. Remove the squash from the oven and let it cool for 5 minutes. Place the squash in a food processor, pulse until pureed, and add the heavy cream and bourbon. Puree until the squash is smooth. Transfer the squash to a large bowl, stir in the butter and Parmesan, and taste. Adjust the seasoning as necessary and set the squash aside.

3. Add the canola oil to a small skillet and warm it over medium-high heat. Add the sage and fry until it is just crispy, 15 to 30 seconds. Remove the sage from the pan and let it drain on a paper towel–lined plate.

4. Garnish the squash with the crispy sage leaves and additional Parmesan.

CREAMY SCOTCH & MUSHROOM
SAUCE, SEE PAGE 148

YIELD: **1 CUP**

ACTIVE TIME: **10 MINUTES**

TOTAL TIME: **20 MINUTES**

CREAMY SCOTCH & MUSHROOM SAUCE

Top a grilled steak with a spoonful or two of this delightfully complex sauce.

1 tablespoon unsalted butter

1 onion, finely diced

2 handfuls of sliced baby bella mushrooms

3 oz. Monkey Shoulder Scotch Whisky

⅔ cup heavy cream

Salt and pepper, to taste

1. Place the butter in a skillet and melt it over medium heat. Add the onion and cook, stirring occasionally, until it has softened, about 5 minutes. Place the onion in a blender and puree until smooth.

2. Add the mushrooms to the skillet and cook, stirring once or twice, until they are browned, about 8 minutes. Stir the Scotch and onion puree into the pan and cook until the alcohol has cooked off.

3. Stir in the cream, season the sauce with salt and pepper, and cook until the sauce turns a light brown.

YIELD: **4 SERVINGS**

ACTIVE TIME: **20 MINUTES**

TOTAL TIME: **2 HOURS**

COURTESY OF TAMARA WAGNER

FRUITY BELL PEPPER & TOMATO SOUP

Although often mislabeled as vegetables, tomatoes and peppers are fruits. With that in mind, pairing with the fruity, full-bodied Mackmyra Mack Swedish Single Malt makes plenty of sense.

1 tablespoon extra-virgin olive oil

1 small onion, chopped

½ lb. tomatoes, chopped

½ red bell pepper, chopped

Flesh of ½ mango, chopped

1¼ cups Vegetable Stock (see page 248)

Salt and pepper, to taste

1. Place the olive oil in a small saucepan and warm it over medium heat. Add the onion and cook, stirring occasionally, until it is translucent, about 3 minutes.

2. Add the tomatoes, bell pepper, and mango and cook, stirring occasionally, for 3 to 4 minutes.

3. Add the stock, scrape up any browned bits from the bottom of the pan, and simmer the soup for 10 minutes.

4. Place the soup in a blender and puree until smooth. Return the soup to the saucepan and bring it to a boil. Remove the pan from heat, season the soup with salt and pepper, and let it cool completely.

5. Chill the soup in the refrigerator for at least 1 hour before serving.

COURTESY OF MICHTER'S DISTILLERY

MAPLE & RYE GLAZE

Roast some root vegetables, brush them with this glaze when they have about 20 minutes left, and you've got an easy, unforgettable side dish.

3 tablespoons unsalted butter

⅓ cup maple syrup

⅓ cup Michter's US*1 Rye Whiskey

1 teaspoon cinnamon

¼ teaspoon cayenne pepper

2 tablespoons fresh thyme

1. Combine all of the ingredients, except for the thyme, in a small saucepan and warm the mixture over medium heat, stirring occasionally. Bring the mixture to a boil, remove the pan from heat, stir in the thyme, and use as desired.

YIELD: **6 SERVINGS**

ACTIVE TIME: **30 MINUTES**

TOTAL TIME: **2 HOURS AND 30 MINUTES**

COURTESY OF TAMARA WAGNER

PEANUT & LENTIL SOUP

Pair with Mackmyra Svensk Ek Swedish Single Malt. This pairing follows the contrasting path. With potatoes, peanuts, and lentils at the heart of this soup, the spicy Svensk Ek stands apart and pulls the best out of each.

3¼ cups Vegetable Stock
(see page 248)

1 potato, peeled and chopped

1 carrot, peeled and chopped

¼ cup red lentils

3 tablespoons chopped fresh chives

2 tablespoons peanut butter

2 tablespoons chopped roasted, unsalted peanuts

Salt and pepper, to taste

1. Place 2½ cups of stock in a saucepan and bring it to a simmer over medium heat. Add the potato, carrot, and lentils and simmer, stirring occasionally, until the potato and lentils have softened, about 10 minutes.

2. Stir in the chives and peanut butter and simmer until the potato and lentils are tender, 6 to 8 minutes, stirring occasionally.

3. Place the soup in a blender and puree until smooth. Place the soup in a mixing bowl, stir in the peanuts and remaining stock, and season the soup with salt and pepper. Let the soup cool to room temperature.

4. Place the soup in the refrigerator and chill for at least 1 hour before serving.

ENTREES

As you've seen, whiskey can be incorporated into just about every occasion where food is the focus, whether it be as ingredient or accompaniment. That said, the majority of your efforts to utilize whiskey in your cooking are going to center around the main course.

As it should be. It's nice to find a perfect match for an appetizer or dessert offering, but when you are able to enhance an entree with your knowledge, the satisfaction becomes palpable, deepening your already considerable appreciation for this unique spirit.

YIELD: **4 SERVINGS**

ACTIVE TIME: **1 HOUR**

TOTAL TIME: **3 HOURS AND 30 MINUTES**

CHICKEN & RICE
WITH BEER VINEGAR AND PRESERVED TRUFFLE

First, Starward Two Fold makes a good pairing because it is used in the glaze of this dish, but that is just one element of a much larger picture. Beyond that, Two Fold balances a malty honeyed and berry sweet side with spicy and earthy, woody elements, all of which mirror the dish well.

For the Chicken Wings

2 oz. salt

1 oz. sugar

2 cups hot water (160°F)

1 oz. garlic cloves

3½ oz. chopped onion

6⅓ cups ice water

8 chicken wing flats, deboned, wing tips left on

2 tablespoons canola oil

Crispy Chicken Skins (see page 252), for garnish

Fresh chives, chopped, for garnish

For the Chicken Mousse

5¼ oz. boneless, skinless chicken breast, diced

½ oz. kosher salt, plus more to taste

½ cup milk

2 oz. crème fraîche

2 oz. heavy cream

2 oz. smoked ham, diced

¾ oz. black truffles, chopped

For the Beer & Whisky Glaze

2⅔ oz. stout malt vinegar

3½ oz. Chicken Stock (see page 245)

¾ oz. sugar

1 oz. Starward Two Fold Australian Whisky

For the Truffle Rice

4¾ oz. sushi rice, soaked in 4¼ cups cold water

¾ cup water

½ cup Chicken Stock

1 tablespoon chicken fat

¼ cup sushi vinegar

2 tablespoons white soy sauce

⅓ oz. sliced scallions

⅓ oz. slivered almonds, toasted, plus more for garnish

⅕ oz. sunflower seeds, toasted, plus more for garnish

1/10 oz. sesame seeds, toasted, plus more for garnish

⅓ oz. black truffles, chopped

1. To begin preparations for the chicken wings, place the salt, sugar, and hot water in a large saucepan and whisk until the salt and sugar have dissolved. Place the garlic and onion in a blender, add some of the ice water, and puree until smooth. Strain the puree into the saucepan, add the remaining ice water and chicken wings, and brine for 2 hours. Remove the chicken wings from the brine, rinse them well, and pat them dry with paper towels.

2. To prepare the chicken mousse, season the chicken with salt and place it in a blender. Puree until it is a smooth paste. Add the milk, crème fraîche, and heavy cream and puree until smooth. Transfer the mousse to a bowl, add the ham and truffles, and fold to incorporate them. Chill the mousse in the refrigerator.

3. To prepare the beer & whisky glaze, place the vinegar, stock, and sugar in a saucepan and bring the mixture to a boil. Cook until the mixture is very syrupy and has reduced by about three-quarters. Remove the pan from the heat, stir in the whisky, and set the glaze aside.

4. To prepare the truffle rice, drain the rice and rinse it well. Place the rice in a rice cooker with the water and the stock. Cook on the sushi rice setting. Place the cooked rice in a mixing bowl, stir in the remaining ingredients, and set the rice aside.

5. Preheat the oven to 325°F. Place the chicken mousse in a piping bag fitted with a fine tip and pipe the mousse into the chicken wings.

6. Place the canola oil in a large skillet and warm it over medium-high heat. Add the wings and sear until they are crispy and golden brown on both sides, about 6 minutes. Place the chicken wings on a baking sheet, brush them with some of the glaze, and place them in the oven. Bake the chicken wings until they are cooked through, about 8 minutes, brushing them frequently with the glaze.

7. Remove the chicken wings from the oven. To serve, spoon the rice into a serving dish and garnish with additional toasted almonds and seeds. Place the chicken wings in a separate serving dish, crumble the Crispy Chicken Skins over them, and garnish with chives.

For the Glazed Endive

1¾ oz. unsalted butter

2 Belgian endives, halved lengthwise

1 oz. sugar

½ cup Chicken Stock (see page 245)

Zest of 1 orange

2 garlic cloves

1 sprig of fresh thyme

For the Quince Aioli

1 quince, peel and seeds removed, cubed

½ cup sugar

8 cups water

1 garlic clove, grated

⅓ oz. kosher salt

¼ cup extra-virgin olive oil

For the Duck Sauce

1½ tablespoons canola oil

Reserved duck back, neck, and wings, roughly chopped

3 shallots, sliced

2 garlic cloves, crushed

2 sprigs of fresh thyme

½ cup Starward Two Fold Australian Whisky

¾ cup red wine

1½ cups duck stock

1¾ oz. unsalted butter

Salt, to taste

For the Honey Gastrique

½ cup orange blossom honey

2 tablespoons Banyuls red wine vinegar

¼ cup Starward Two Fold Australian Whisky

⅕ oz. kosher salt

For the Duck

4 to 5 lb. Crown of 21-Day Dry-Aged Peking Duck (preferably from Sonoma County Liberty Ducks), trimmed, back, neck, and wings reserved

YIELD: **6 SERVINGS**

ACTIVE TIME: **1 HOUR AND 30 MINUTES**

TOTAL TIME: **2 HOURS**

COURTESY OF CHEF JOSIAH CITRIN

LIBERTY DUCK
WITH QUINCE AIOLI & ENDIVE

The rich flavor of duck needs something bold to stand against it, and Starward Two Fold more than meets that call.

1. To prepare the glazed endive, place the butter in a large skillet and melt it over medium heat. Add the endives, cut sides down, and sear until they are golden brown. Add the sugar and stir until it forms a light caramel. Deglaze the pan with the stock, scraping any browned bits from the bottom of the pan. Add the orange zest, garlic, and thyme, bring the dish to a light simmer, and cook for 6 minutes. Remove the pan from heat and let the endives cool in the cooking liquid.

2. To prepare the quince aioli, place the quince in a saucepan with the sugar and water. Bring to a boil and cook the quince until it is soft. Drain, place the quince in a blender, and add the remaining ingredients. Puree until smooth, strain, and set the aioli aside.

3. To prepare the duck sauce, warm a large cast-iron skillet over high heat. Add the canola oil and the chopped duck trimmings and cook, stirring occasionally, until golden brown. Add the shallots, garlic, and thyme and cook, stirring frequently, for 3 minutes. Deglaze the pan with 3½ oz. of the whisky, scraping up any browned bits from the bottom of the pan. When the alcohol has cooked off, add the red wine and cook until the liquid in the pan is syrupy. Stir in the stock and

simmer for 20 minutes. Strain the mixture through a fine-mesh sieve and place the sauce in a clean saucepan. Bring the sauce to a simmer and cook until it has reduced to the desired consistency. Gently stir in the butter and season the sauce with salt. Stir in the remaining whisky and set the sauce aside.

4. To prepare the honey gastrique, place all of the ingredients in a medium saucepan and bring the mixture to a boil. Remove the pan from heat and let the gastrique cool.

5. Preheat the oven to 360°F. To prepare the duck, brush the crown of duck with the honey gastrique. Place the duck in a roasting pan, place it in the oven, and roast until it is cooked through, about 18 minutes. Remove the duck from the oven and let it rest for 15 minutes.

6. To serve, slice the duck and place it on a plate, just off center. Place the glazed endive on the other side of the plate. Spoon the duck sauce into the center of the plate. Place the quince aioli in a piping bag fitted with a fine tip and pipe small dots of the aioli onto the endive. Pipe and then smear a small amount of quince aioli around the edge of the plate.

YIELD: **6 SERVINGS**

ACTIVE TIME: **45 MINUTES**

TOTAL TIME: **5 HOURS**

PORK BELLY BURNT ENDS

This recipe utilizes apple and honey flavors atop the brown sugar, which really calls for a wheated bourbon to accompany it. That said, the spice rub is so spicy that said wheated bourbon should not go too far down the soft and floral path, which is why Larceny is the one to reach for.

For the Rub

½ cup paprika

½ cup chili powder

½ cup brown sugar

¼ cup black pepper

¼ cup kosher salt

2 tablespoons garlic powder

2 tablespoons onion powder

1 tablespoon mustard powder

1 tablespoon cayenne pepper

1 tablespoon cumin

For the Pork Belly

1 slab of pork belly, skin removed

1 cup unsalted butter

½ cup packed brown sugar

½ cup honey

6 tablespoons Tiger Sauce

1 cup barbecue sauce

¼ cup apple juice

¼ cup apple jelly

1. To prepare the rub, place all of the ingredients in a large mixing bowl and stir until thoroughly combined. Set the rub aside and start to prepare the pork belly. This rub will keep in an airtight container in a cool, dry place for up to 6 months.

2. Preheat an indirect smoker to 250°F. Set a wire rack in a rimmed baking sheet. To begin preparations for the pork belly, cut the pork belly into 1-inch cubes and place it in a mixing bowl. Generously season the pork belly with the rub, toss until coated, and place it on the wire rack.

3. Place the pork belly in the smoker and cook for 2 hours, which will keep the pork belly tender while also caramelizing the exterior.

4. Remove the pork belly from the smoker and place it in an aluminum pan. Add the butter, brown sugar, honey, and ¼ cup of the Tiger Sauce, stir to coat the pork belly, and cover the pan with aluminum foil. Place the pork belly back in the smoker and cook for another 2 hours.

5. Remove the pork belly from the smoker and drain the liquid from the pan. Set the pork belly aside.

6. Place the barbecue sauce, apple juice, apple jelly, and the remaining Tiger Sauce in a saucepan and cook over medium heat, stirring occasionally, until the jelly has liquefied.

7. Add the glaze to the pork belly, toss until it is coated, and return it to the smoker. Cook until the pork belly is crispy and the glaze has caramelized, 7 to 10 minutes. Remove the pork belly from the smoker and enjoy.

YIELD: **6 SERVINGS**

ACTIVE TIME: **45 MINUTES**

TOTAL TIME: **6 HOURS AND 30 MINUTES**

IRISH WHISKEY–GLAZED RIBS

The crisp, well-balanced flavor of Egan's makes it a natural to incorporate in your cooking.

3 lbs. baby back pork ribs

Salt and pepper, to taste

2 tablespoons extra-virgin olive oil

1 small onion, minced

2 garlic cloves, minced

2 teaspoons cumin

2 teaspoons smoked paprika

1 teaspoon cayenne pepper (optional)

2 oz. Egan's Conviction Irish Whiskey

3 tablespoons honey

2 tablespoons ketchup

1. If your butcher has not already done so, remove the thin membrane from the back of the ribs. Place the ribs in a large roasting pan or baking dish and season them generously with salt and pepper. Let the ribs rest at room temperature.

2. Place the olive oil in a small saucepan and warm it over medium heat. Add the onion and cook, stirring occasionally, until it has softened, about 5 minutes.

3. Add the garlic, cumin, paprika, and cayenne (if desired) and cook, stirring continually, for 2 minutes.

4. Add the whiskey and cook, scraping up any browned bits from the bottom of the pan, for 1 minute. Remove the pan from heat, stir in the honey and ketchup, and then pour the glaze over the ribs.

5. Cover the dish with aluminum foil and chill the ribs in the refrigerator for at least 3 hours, and up to 24 hours.

6. Preheat the oven to 300°F. Place the ribs in the oven and cook them, covered with foil, for 2½ hours.

7. Remove the foil, baste the ribs with the pan juices, and raise the heat to 400°F. Cook until the glaze on the ribs is crispy, about 20 minutes.

8. Remove the ribs from the oven, pour the pan juices into a small saucepan, and bring the juices to a boil over high heat. Cook until the liquid has reduced and serve the reduction alongside the ribs.

YIELD: **1 DRINK**
ACTIVE TIME: **2 MINUTES**
TOTAL TIME: **2 MINUTES**

COURTESY OF JOSHUA BROWN,
Manager at J. Render's Southern Table & Bar,
Lexington, Kentucky

THE STAGGER LEE

"At the restaurant I enjoy pairing the Stagger Lee with our smoked baby back ribs. The cocktail has nice hints of citrus, baking spices, and caramel. I find that these layers of flavor perfectly complement the smoke and salt of our ribs," says Brown.

1½ oz. bourbon

½ oz. Aperol

1 oz. Vya Sweet Vermouth

3 dashes of Regan's Orange Bitters

1 orange twist, for garnish

1. Place all of the ingredients, except for the garnish, in a mixing glass, fill it two-thirds of the way with ice, and stir for approximately 30 revolutions.

2. Strain the cocktail into a coupe and garnish with the orange twist.

YIELD: **6 SERVINGS**

ACTIVE TIME: **20 MINUTES**

TOTAL TIME: **1 HOUR AND 15 MINUTES**

COURTESY OF CHEF KEVIN TEMPLETON,
BarleyMash, San Diego, California

BROWN SUGAR RIBS

Pair with Wild Turkey 101 Bourbon. These ribs have plenty of sweetness and spice atop that fat, succulent pork. That calls for a bold bourbon, but not one so bold it overpowers the food. The Bird smartly fits that niche.

2 racks of baby back pork ribs

2 cups brown sugar

2 tablespoons kosher salt

2 tablespoons freshly ground black pepper

2 tablespoons ancho chile powder (optional)

1 lb. bacon fat, chilled or at room temperature

Barbecue sauce, for serving

1. Preheat your gas or charcoal grill, setting up one zone for direct heat and one for indirect heat. If your butcher has not already done so, remove the thin membrane from the back of each rack of ribs.

2. In a small bowl, combine the brown sugar, salt, pepper, and chile powder (if desired). Generously rub the mixture on both sides of ribs, and then coat the ribs with the bacon fat. Place 2 to 3 layers of heavy-duty aluminum foil down, place the racks of ribs, side by side, on top of the foil, and securely wrap the ribs, making sure there are no holes or tears in the foil. Crimp the edges of the packet to seal.

3. Place the packet over indirect heat and cook until the ribs are falling off the bone, 30 to 40 minutes, turning them every 5 minutes.

4. Remove the packet from the grill. Carefully open it, remove the ribs, and discard the rendered fat and foil. Place the ribs over direct heat and grill until charred on each side.

5. Remove the ribs from the grill and serve with barbecue sauce.

A BROWN: A COCKTAIL AND A STORY

BY GEORGE MOTZ, TELEVISION PERSONALITY, AUTHOR, HISTORIAN, FILMMAKER, NOTED BURGER GURU

I love burgers and I love whiskey. Put the two together and I'm happy. And, if we are grilling burgers outside, and drinking whiskey with family, I'm in heaven.

The moment grill smoke hits my senses I'm in search of a drink. I'm not really sure about the science that triggers the response, but it's real, as you probably know. In all likelihood, there is a fair amount of sense-memory involved, as I think about all of the good times I've had sitting outdoors on cool nights, grilling, eating, and drinking with my Southern family.

My mama is from Awendaw, South Carolina, but moved to New York to raise a family. I still go back to visit her extended family at least three or four times a year, and that still doesn't feel like enough. We roast oysters, enjoy dishes featuring local Lowcountry shrimp, grill burgers, play guitar, and generally have a great time.

Once I was old enough to join my uncles around the fire, I was introduced to the family cocktail: A Brown.

The "A" is important because "brown" alone would refer only to the whiskey at hand in my family vernacular, as in "Don't forget to pack the brown," or "Give me a splash of brown." In this case the name implies you need a drink. "I could sure go for A Brown right now," likely means the grill is smoking, and it's time to start the party.

A Brown is simple, and you will recognize the cocktail immediately because it's similar to a Jack 'n' Ginger, or a 7&7.

First, head out into the fresh Southern air. If you can't do that, just go out in the backyard and start grilling anything. Next, get a 16 oz. red Solo cup and fill it to the brim with ice cubes. Pour a few glugs of your favorite bourbon over the ice—for my family it's Evan Williams only—then fill the rest of the cup with any clear soda such as Sprite, Slice, or, best of all, ginger ale. Stir with a finger and enjoy. The ratios will vary as the night moves on, as they should. Go forth, and make great memories with good food and family.

YIELD: **4 SERVINGS**

ACTIVE TIME: **25 MINUTES**

TOTAL TIME: **45 MINUTES**

GRILLED SWORDFISH
WITH CHERMOULA SAUCE & COUSCOUS

Chermoula will add plenty of zing to this dish, which checks every possible box when paired with Willett Pot Still Reserve Bourbon. The whiskey here needs to provide elements that complement the other three elements, as contrasting them would be too much. One thing about Willett is how well it balances the traditional sweet and spicy aspects of bourbon, so there is something in it for every inch of this platter.

For the Couscous

2 tablespoons extra-virgin olive oil

1 garlic clove, chopped

½ red onion, diced

1 tablespoon smoked paprika

1½ teaspoons ground ginger

1 teaspoon cumin

2 teaspoons turmeric

¼ cup dried currants

1 teaspoon hot sauce

¼ cup tomato puree

½ cup Israeli couscous

1¼ cups Vegetable or Chicken Stock (see page 248 or 245)

1 teaspoon kosher salt

For the Swordfish

2 to 4 (6 oz.) swordfish fillets

Salt, to taste

1½ teaspoons Aleppo pepper

1½ teaspoons sumac

Extra-virgin olive oil, as needed

For the Chermoula Sauce

Zest and juice of 1 orange

Zest and juice of 1 lemon

Zest and juice of 1 lime

1 teaspoon cumin

½ garlic clove, chopped

1 tablespoon chopped fresh mint

½ cup chopped fresh cilantro

½ teaspoon Aleppo pepper

2 teaspoons chopped shallot

¾ cup extra-virgin olive oil

1. To prepare the couscous, place the olive oil in a medium saucepan and warm it over medium heat. Add the garlic, red onion, paprika, ginger, cumin, and turmeric and cook, stirring frequently, for 2 minutes. Stir in the remaining ingredients, bring the mixture to a boil, and cover the pan. Remove the pan from heat and let it sit for 5 minutes. Remove the lid, fluff the couscous with a fork, and set it aside.

2. To prepare the chermoula sauce, place all of the ingredients in a mixing bowl and whisk until well combined. Store in the refrigerator until ready to use.

3. Prepare a gas or charcoal grill for medium heat (about 400°F). To prepare the swordfish, season both sides of the fillets with salt, Aleppo pepper, and sumac. Brush the grates with olive oil and place the swordfish on the grill. Grill until well seared on both sides and cooked through (internal temperature of about 110°F), about 6 minutes, turning the fillets just once.

4. To serve, place a spoonful of the couscous salad on a plate. Top the couscous with the swordfish and spoon the chermoula over the top.

NEW YORK SOUR TENDERLOIN,
SEE PAGE 174

COURTESY OF GARRISON BROTHERS DISTILLERY

NEW YORK SOUR TENDERLOIN

Don't hesitate to extend the reach of this compound butter to every steak that hits your grill.

For the Tenderloin

½ cup Garrison Brothers Small Batch Bourbon

¼ cup balsamic vinegar

2 tablespoons fresh lemon juice

2 tablespoons Simple Syrup (see page 253)

1 center-cut beef tenderloin

Salt and pepper, to taste

Balsamic Glaze (see page 257), for garnish

Roasted potatoes, for serving

Blanched or steamed broccoli, for serving

For the Compound Butter

2 tablespoons Garrison Brothers Small Batch Bourbon

1 cup unsalted butter, softened

2 garlic cloves, minced

1 tablespoon chopped fresh rosemary

1 tablespoon chopped fresh thyme

1. To begin preparations for the tenderloin, place the bourbon, balsamic vinegar, lemon juice, and syrup in a bowl and stir to combine. Place the tenderloin in a resealable plastic bag, add the marinade, and shake the bag until the tenderloin is evenly coated. Place the tenderloin in the refrigerator and let it marinate for 4 to 6 hours.

2. To prepare the compound butter, place all of the ingredients in the work bowl of a stand mixer fitted with the paddle attachment and beat the mixture until well combined. Store the compound butter in the refrigerator.

3. Preheat the oven to 350°F. Remove the tenderloin from the marinade and pat it dry with paper towels. Place 2 tablespoons of the compound butter in a large cast-iron skillet and melt it over medium-high heat. Season the tenderloin with salt and pepper, place it in the pan, and sear until browned all over, about 2 minutes per side.

4. Spread the rest of the compound butter over the tenderloin and place the pan in the oven. Roast the tenderloin for 20 to 25 minutes for medium-rare, basting it occasionally with the compound butter.

5. Remove the tenderloin from the oven and let it rest for 15 minutes.

6. Slice the tenderloin, drizzle some Balsamic Glaze over the top, and serve with potatoes and broccoli.

YIELD: **2 SERVINGS**

ACTIVE TIME: **40 MINUTES**

TOTAL TIME: **1 HOUR**

COURTESY OF GARRISON BROTHERS DISTILLERY

BOURBON & CIDER-GLAZED SALMON

As you probably already know, coating salmon in a sweet glaze and crisping it up in a cast-iron skillet is a surefire winner.

1 cup apple cider

2 tablespoons apple cider vinegar

¼ cup soy sauce

¼ cup sugar

¼ cup Garrison Brothers Small Batch Bourbon

½ lb. rainbow carrots, peeled

5 tablespoons unsalted butter

2 (6 oz.) salmon fillets, deboned

Salt and pepper, to taste

1 tablespoon honey

½ teaspoon freshly grated nutmeg

¼ teaspoon cardamom

¼ teaspoon ground cloves

½ teaspoon coriander

Brussels sprouts, for serving

1. Place the apple cider, apple cider vinegar, soy sauce, and sugar in a saucepan and bring to a simmer over medium heat, stirring occasionally. Cook until the mixture has reduced by half, 15 to 20 minutes. Stir in the bourbon and simmer until the mixture has reduced to about ½ cup, about 10 minutes. Remove the pan from heat and set the glaze aside.

2. Bring water to a boil in a medium saucepan and prepare an ice bath. Place the carrots in the boiling water, blanch for 1 minute, and then plunge them into the ice bath. Drain the carrots, pat them dry, and set them aside.

3. Place 2 tablespoons of the butter in a cast-iron skillet and melt it over medium-high heat. Season the salmon fillets with salt and pepper, place them in the pan, and sear until golden brown, 3 to 4 minutes. Turn the salmon over, pour the glaze over the top, and reduce the heat to medium. Cook until the salmon is cooked through, frequently basting the fillets with the glaze.

4. While the salmon is cooking, place the remaining butter in a large skillet and melt it over medium-high heat. Add the carrots, honey, nutmeg, cardamom, cloves, and coriander, season the carrots with salt, and cook, stirring frequently, until the carrots are cooked through and nicely coated, 4 to 5 minutes.

5. Serve the salmon alongside the carrots and Brussels sprouts.

YIELD: **6 TO 8 SERVINGS**

ACTIVE TIME: **20 MINUTES**

TOTAL TIME: **3 HOURS**

BOURBON-GLAZED HAM

A dish that is simple enough to prepare on a busy weeknight, and exceptional enough to serve as the centerpiece of a holiday gathering.

1 bone-in ham

¼ cup Garrison Brothers Small Batch Bourbon

1 cup molasses

1 cup brown sugar

¼ cup Dijon mustard

1 teaspoon cinnamon

1 teaspoon ground cloves

1. Preheat the oven to 275°F. Place the ham in a roasting pan, cover it with aluminum foil, place it in the oven, and cook until the ham is heated through, about 2 hours.

2. Place the bourbon, molasses, brown sugar, Dijon mustard, cinnamon, and cloves in a medium saucepan and warm the mixture over medium heat, stirring frequently, until the sugar has dissolved, about 3 minutes.

3. Brush the glaze over the ham and raise the oven's temperature to 350°F. Return the ham to the oven and cook, uncovered, until the glaze has caramelized, about 30 minutes.

4. Remove the ham from the oven and let it rest for 10 minutes before slicing and serving.

YIELD: **4 SERVINGS**

ACTIVE TIME: **1 HOUR**

TOTAL TIME: **2 HOURS**

COURTESY OF STU PLUSH, Executive Chef at Bardstown Bourbon Company

ORANGE & HONEY–GLAZED STUFFED QUAIL

Plush recommends using unsweetened cornbread for the stuffing, as his recommended pairing—Bardstown Fusion Series #7—is a well-seasoned caramel bomb.

For the Quail

1 cup orange juice

2 tablespoons brown sugar

2 tablespoons honey

1 tablespoon apple cider vinegar

Pinch of red pepper flakes

4 whole, semiboneless quail

Roasted potatoes, for serving

Collard Greens (see page 260), for serving

For the Cornbread Stuffing

½ cup unsalted butter, plus more as needed

½ lb. andouille sausage, finely diced

1 Granny Smith apple, peeled and finely diced

½ onion, minced

2 celery stalks, minced

1 teaspoon minced fresh sage

Salt and pepper, to taste

1½ cups Chicken Stock (see page 245)

1 large egg

¼ cup chopped fresh parsley

3 cups day-old Brioche (see page 241; ½-inch cubes)

3 cups day-old Cornbread (see page 244; ½-inch cubes)

1. To begin preparations for the quail, combine all of the ingredients, except for the quail and those designated for serving, in a small saucepan and bring the mixture to a boil. Reduce the heat and simmer until the glaze has reduced by about half.

2. Preheat the oven to 375°F. Coat a 2-quart baking dish with butter. To begin preparations for the stuffing, place 1 tablespoon of the butter in a large skillet and melt it over medium heat. Add the sausage and cook, stirring occasionally, until browned. Transfer the sausage to a bowl.

3. Place the remaining butter in the skillet, add the apple, onion, celery, and sage, season the mixture with salt and pepper, and cook, stirring occasionally, until the vegetables are tender, about 5 minutes. Add the stock and bring to a simmer. Remove the pan from heat.

4. Place the egg and parsley in a large bowl and whisk to combine. Add the brioche, cornbread, sausage, and vegetable mixture and stir until combined. Pour the stuffing into the baking dish, cover it with aluminum foil, and place it in the oven. Bake for 30 minutes, remove from the oven, and let the stuffing cool slightly.

5. Raise the oven's temperature to 400°F. Place a rack in a large roasting pan. Stuff each quail with the cornbread stuffing and place them on the rack. Brush the quail generously with the glaze, place them in the oven, and roast until a thermometer inserted into the center of the stuffing registers 155°F.

6. Remove the quail from the oven, spoon more glaze over the top, and serve with potatoes and Collard Greens.

BARDSTOWN BOURBON COMPANY

With the help of renowned distiller Steve Nally, Bardstown Bourbon Company opened in 2016 as a contract producer for other brands. The demand for those services has been strong; just a year and a half after starting production, they found it necessary to install a second, 50-foot-tall column still. According to Nally, the company is producing 30 different mash bills for almost two dozen clients, on top of its own whiskeys.

With its current production of 100,000 barrels of bourbon per year, Bardstown are one of the top ten privately owned distilleries, by volume, in the country. So far, they have been releasing blends under their own label, and plan to start releasing individual bottlings when their whiskeys reach six years of age, either this year or the next. In the meantime, enjoy Bardstown's blends, which are are super-smooth and sophisticated.

YIELD: **6 SERVINGS**

ACTIVE TIME: **30 MINUTES**

TOTAL TIME: **1 HOUR**

BOURBON & PORK CHILI

As we know, chili can accommodate almost any whim. Adding the pepper-laced char of Old Grand-Dad makes the most of that welcoming nature.

1 lb. ground pork

1 large or 2 medium red bell peppers, stems and seeds removed, diced

1 onion, diced

3 garlic cloves, minced

2 (14 oz.) cans of kidney beans, with their liquid

1 (14 oz.) can of diced tomatoes, drained

1 cup Tomato Sauce (see page 261)

2 tablespoons chipotle chile powder

2 tablespoons sugar

1 tablespoon cinnamon

1 teaspoon black pepper

2 oz. Old Grand-Dad Bourbon

1. Place the ground pork in a large saucepan and cook it over medium heat until it is browned, about 8 minutes, breaking it up with a wooden spoon as it cooks. Drain the majority of the fat from the pan.

2. Stir in the bell peppers, onion, and garlic and cook, stirring occasionally, until the vegetables have softened, about 8 minutes.

3. Add the remaining ingredients, stir until well combined, and bring the chili to a boil. Reduce the heat to low, cover the pan, and simmer the chili until the flavor has developed to your liking, about 30 minutes.

4. Ladle the chili into warmed bowls and enjoy.

COURTESY OF MICHTER'S DISTILLERY

BRAISED SHORT RIBS
WITH HORSERADISH MASHED POTATOES

This a well-seasoned platter, with the herbs and the horseradish. Yet it is also savory, and the best way to straddle that combination is a Kentucky-style rye like Michter's US*1 Rye Whiskey.

For the Short Ribs

¼ cup extra-virgin olive oil

3½ to 4 lbs. bone-in beef short ribs

Salt and pepper, to taste

1 large Vidalia onion, chopped

1 lb. carrots, peeled and chopped

5 garlic cloves, minced

2 tablespoons tomato paste

3½ to 4 cups Beef Stock (see page 246)

½ cup prunes

20 sprigs of fresh thyme, tied together

20 sprigs of fresh rosemary, tied together

For the Mashed Potatoes

5 large russet potatoes, peeled and cut into 1-inch cubes

¼ cup heavy cream

4 to 6 tablespoons prepared horseradish

4 tablespoons unsalted butter

1 to 2 teaspoons kosher salt

½ teaspoon freshly ground black pepper

1. Preheat the oven to 300°F. To begin preparations for the short ribs, place the olive oil in a Dutch oven and warm it over medium-high heat. Generously season the short ribs with salt and pepper. Working in batches to avoid crowding the pot, add the short ribs and sear until they are browned all over. Remove the seared short ribs from the pot and place them on a plate.

2. Add the onion and carrots and cook, stirring frequently, until they start to soften, about 5 minutes. Add the garlic and cook, stirring continually, for 1 minute. Stir in the tomato paste and cook for another minute.

3. Return the short ribs to the pot, add stock until the short ribs are covered three-quarters of the way, and add the prunes and fresh herbs. Cover the Dutch oven, place it in the oven, and braise the short ribs until they are very tender, about 2½ hours.

4. While short ribs are in the oven, begin preparations for the mashed potatoes. Bring water to a boil in a large saucepan. Add the potatoes and cook until tender, 10 to 15 minutes.

5. Drain the potatoes and place them in a large mixing bowl. Mash the potatoes until smooth, stir in the cream, ¼ cup of the prepared horseradish, butter, salt, and pepper. Taste and add more horseradish if desired.

6. Remove the short ribs from the oven and serve them alongside the mashed potatoes.

YIELD: **12 SERVINGS**

ACTIVE TIME: **10 MINUTES**

TOTAL TIME: **9 HOURS**

COURTESY OF PEGGY NOE STEVENS,
originally published in her book, *Which Fork Do I Use With My Bourbon?*

GRANNY HUNTER'S BOURBON TENDERLOIN

This elegant entree comes from Peggy's mother-in-law, who entertained on the family farm in Bourbon County, Kentucky. You can substitute pork tenderloin for the beef—just sear the pork in a skillet before roasting it at 350°F for 30 minutes per pound.

2 tablespoons Kentucky bourbon

¾ cup canola oil

½ cup soy sauce

⅓ cup packed brown sugar

¼ cup red wine vinegar

2 garlic cloves, peeled and minced

2 teaspoons ground ginger

½ teaspoon coriander

5 to 6 lb. beef tenderloin

1. Place all of the ingredients in a large roasting pan and stir to combine. Place the pan in the refrigerator and let the tenderloin marinate for 8 hours.

2. Preheat the oven to 425°F. Remove the tenderloin from the refrigerator and pour the marinade into a saucepan. Bring it to a boil and cook for 5 minutes. Pour the marinade over the tenderloin, place the tenderloin in the oven, and roast for 30 minutes.

3. Reduce the heat to 375°F and roast until the tenderloin is cooked through, about 20 minutes. Remove from the oven and let the tenderloin rest for 10 minutes before slicing and serving alongside the pan juices.

YIELD: **4 SERVINGS**

ACTIVE TIME: **20 MINUTES**

TOTAL TIME: **1 HOUR**

COURTESY OF CHEF MARTIN RIVERA
FOR HANSON OF SONOMA DISTILLERY

HANSON'S WHISKEY AU POIVRE

A French classic gets an innovative updating that would make even the staunchest traditionalists rethink things.

2 (10 oz). New York strip steaks

Salt, to taste

1½ tablespoons whole black peppercorns

2 tablespoons canola oil

4 garlic cloves, 2 minced, 2 left whole

3 sprigs of fresh thyme

3 tablespoons unsalted butter, chilled and diced

1 shallot, minced

⅓ cup Hanson of Sonoma's Single Malt Whiskey

1½ cups heavy cream

1. Pat the steaks dry and season them generously with salt. Let the steaks rest at room temperature for 30 minutes.

2. Place the peppercorns in a dry skillet and toast them until they just start to smoke, about 2 minutes. Remove them from the pan and use a mortar and pestle to coarsely grind the peppercorns.

3. Place the canola oil in a cast-iron skillet and warm it over high heat. Pat the steaks dry and place them in the pan. Sear until golden brown on both sides, about 6 minutes.

4. Reduce the heat to medium-low, add the whole garlic cloves, thyme, and 1 tablespoon of butter. Cook the steaks, while basting them, for about 2 minutes for medium-rare. Remove the steaks from the pan and let them rest.

5. Place the shallot, minced garlic, ground peppercorns, and remaining butter in the skillet and cook, stirring frequently, until the shallot and garlic have softened, about 5 minutes. Stir in the whiskey and cook until most of the liquid has evaporated, 1 to 2 minutes. Add the cream, bring the sauce to a simmer, and cook until it thickens slightly, about 1 minute or until it coats the back of a spoon.

6. Slice the steaks against the grain, transfer the slices to a platter, and spoon the sauce over the top.

YIELD: **6 SERVINGS**
ACTIVE TIME: **15 MINUTES**
TOTAL TIME: **45 MINUTES**

CURRY CORN CHOWDER

Pair with Highland Park Valknut, which has a sandalwood current and just a hint of smoke, complementing the Madras curry wonderfully. The finish of the Valknut runs a bit like Constant Comment tea, only building on the effect.

2 tablespoons unsalted butter

2 red potatoes, peeled and chopped

1 yellow onion, chopped

2 tablespoons all-purpose flour

1½ cups canned corn, drained

1½ cups milk

1½ cups Vegetable Stock
(see page 248)

2 tablespoons Madras curry powder

Salt and pepper, to taste

1. Place the butter in a medium saucepan and melt it over medium heat. Add the potatoes and onion and cook, stirring occasionally, until they have softened, about 5 minutes.

2. Sprinkle the flour over the vegetables and cook, stirring continually, for 2 minutes. Add the corn, milk, and stock and stir to incorporate.

3. Stir in the curry powder, season the soup with salt and pepper, and bring it to a boil. Reduce the heat to medium-low, cover the pan, and simmer the soup until the flavor has developed to your liking, 25 to 30 minutes.

4. Ladle the soup into warmed bowls and enjoy.

YIELD: **4 SERVINGS**

ACTIVE TIME: **25 MINUTES**

TOTAL TIME: **50 MINUTES**

FRENCH ONION SOUP

The bold rye spice and vanilla sweetness of Wild Turkey Rye Whiskey 101 will supply the contrast this hearty soup requires.

1 tablespoon unsalted butter

2 tablespoons extra-virgin olive oil

4 red onions, chopped

2 garlic cloves, chopped

Salt, to taste

1 cup red wine

2 tablespoons red wine vinegar

3 cups Beef Stock (see page 246)

2 sprigs of fresh thyme

2 sprigs of fresh parsley

1 bay leaf

4 slices of day-old bread, toasted

Gruyère cheese, shredded, for garnish

1. Place the butter and olive oil in a medium saucepan and warm the mixture over medium-low heat. Add the onions and garlic, season the vegetables with salt, and cook, stirring frequently, until the onions have caramelized, about 20 minutes.

2. Add the wine, raise the heat to medium-high, and cook, scraping up any browned bits from the bottom of the pan, until the wine has reduced and become syrupy.

3. Add the vinegar, stock, and herbs, reduce the heat to medium-low, and simmer the soup for 20 minutes.

4. Remove the herbs and discard them. Preheat the broiler on the oven. Ladle the soup into crocks or oven-safe bowls and top each portion with a slice of bread. Sprinkle the Gruyère over the bread, place the bowls beneath the broiler, and broil until the cheese has melted and is beginning to brown. Remove from the oven and enjoy.

WOODFORD RESERVE

To understand what Woodford Reserve is really all about, one must go to Scotland. In 1993, The Balvenie, one of the distilleries in the William Grant & Sons portfolio, was established as a "boutique" Scotch distillery. Brown-Forman, owner of the famed Jack Daniel's distillery, established Woodford Reserve not long after. The executives at Brown-Forman strategically positioned Woodford as The Balvenie to Jack Daniel's Glenfiddich.

Woodford is meant to be a sophisticated bourbon. Its flavor profile highlights brandy, Cognac, and fruit. More so, master distiller Chris Morris is attempting to make a bourbon that is of a high-enough caliber to dominate internationally. If I were to liken Woodford Reserve to a famous Scotch, it would be Glenmorangie. It has the same Cognac, brandy, honey, and spice notes as the famed Highlands single malt, but the Woodford also has a big dose of caramel up front. Its quotient of rye keeps it from being cloyingly sweet, making for a dryer bourbon without sacrificing its Kentucky heritage.

YIELD: **12 SERVINGS**

ACTIVE TIME: **30 MINUTES**

TOTAL TIME: **1 HOUR AND 15 MINUTES**

COURTESY OF CHEF ADAM COOKE

CORN CHOWDER WITH ANDOUILLE

This also works well as a chilled soup. To serve it chilled, place the pan in an ice bath, stir until it has cooled to room temperature, and refrigerate for 3 hours before serving. Cooke recommends pairing this with Mellow Corn Whiskey, a bonded classic in the corn whiskey realm.

10 ears of corn

16 cups Chicken Stock (see page 245)

2 links of andouille sausage, diced

½ lb. unsalted butter

3 yellow onions, diced

6 celery stalks, chopped

6 red bell peppers, stems and seeds removed, diced

Cloves from 1 head of garlic, diced

¼ cup all-purpose flour

2 potatoes, peeled and diced

Salt and pepper, to taste

4 cups heavy cream

1. Preheat the oven to 450°F. Place the ears of corn in the oven and roast them until the kernels are soft, 20 to 25 minutes. Remove the corn from the oven and let it cool slightly. When the ears of corn are cool enough to handle, shuck them, cut the kernels from the cobs, and place the kernels in a bowl. Reserve the cobs.

2. Place the stock in a large saucepan and warm it over medium-high heat. Milk the corn cobs into the stock and then add them to the stock. Simmer for 30 minutes.

3. While the stock is simmering, place the sausage in a large saucepan and cook it over medium heat, stirring occasionally, until is browned, 6 to 8 minutes. Add the butter, melt it, and then add the onions, celery, and bell peppers. Cook, stirring occasionally, until the vegetables have softened, about 5 minutes.

4. Add the garlic and cook, stirring continually, for 1 minute. Add the flour and cook, stirring continually, for 2 minutes.

5. While whisking continually, gradually add the stock. Bring the soup to a boil, add the corn kernels and potatoes, and reduce the heat so that the soup simmers. Cook until the potatoes are just tender, about 20 minutes.

6. Season the soup with salt and pepper, stir in the heavy cream, and cook until warmed through. Ladle the chowder into warmed bowls and enjoy.

YIELD: **2 SERVINGS**

ACTIVE TIME: **30 MINUTES**

TOTAL TIME: **1 HOUR**

COURTESY OF CHEF REED JOHNSON

COUNTRY HAM–WRAPPED PORK CHOPS WITH BRAISED GREENS

Bourbon is a good fail-safe for pork (and this is pork on pork!), but it's the kale that makes me think of the chewy Woodford Reserve Bourbon and its trademark earthy, almost metallic note.

For the Pork Chops

6 thin slices of country ham

2 center-cut, bone-in pork chops

Salt and pepper, to taste

4 fresh sage leaves

1 tablespoon canola oil

For the Greens

2 tablespoons extra-virgin olive oil

1 Spanish onion, julienned

1 teaspoon red pepper flakes

1 bunch of kale, stems removed, sliced

1 bunch of collard greens, stems removed, sliced

2 cups Ham Stock (see page 247)

Salt and pepper, to taste

2 tablespoons unsalted butter

For the Sauce

4 oz. Apple Butter (see page 262)

2 oz. Ballotin Caramel Turtle Whiskey

1. Preheat the oven to 350°F. To begin preparations for the pork chops, lay out the slices of ham on a counter with the edges overlapping slightly. Pat the pork chops dry and lightly season them with salt and pepper. Place a sage leaf on each side of the pork chops, lay the pork chops on top of the ham, and wrap them tightly.

2. Warm a large cast-iron skillet over high heat. Add the canola oil, warm it, and then add the pork chops. Sear until well browned, about 4 minutes. Turn the pork chops over, place them in the oven, and roast until the centers of the pork chops are 145°F. Remove the pork chops from the oven and remove them from the pan.

3. To prepare the greens, place the olive oil in a large skillet and warm it over medium-high heat. Add the onion and red pepper flakes and cook, stirring occasionally, until the onion is translucent, about 3 minutes. Add the kale and collard greens and cook, stirring occasionally, until they start to wilt, about 2 minutes. Add the stock, season the dish with salt and pepper, and cook until the greens are tender, about 30 minutes. Stir in the butter and serve.

4. To prepare the sauce, place the apple butter and whiskey in the pan used to cook the pork chops and warm over medium heat until the consistency is right.

5. To serve, pile greens on a plate. Place one pork chop against the greens and then drizzle the sauce over the dish.

A NOTE ON ACIDITY

If you're familiar with wine pairings, you may be wondering: Why no talk of acidity? Bringing up acidity with other kinds of food pairings is commonplace. For example, at a wine pairing event you might hear, "We are using this white wine because its acidity cuts right through the fat and salt of that bacon." Beer and wine have a much broader range of acidity than whiskey, with sweet white wines and sour ales running close to the acidity of lemon juice (pH 3). By comparison, whiskeys are more or less as acidic as a cup of coffee (pH 5). As all whiskeys are marginally acidic and sit on a narrow band of the pH scale, acidity just isn't the same factor in pairing with food as it could be for other alcoholic drinks.

YIELD: **10 DRINKS**

ACTIVE TIME: **10 MINUTES**

TOTAL TIME: **3 HOURS AND 45 MINUTES**

COURTESY OF ALEXANDER LOPEZ-WILSON

PEACH SWEET TEA

An easy sipper meant to be enjoyed in the shade while the pleasant scent of meat smoke from the grill whets the palate.

3 peaches, pits removed, diced

8 cups boiling water

6 bags of black tea

1½ cups bourbon

1 cup sugar

1. Place the peaches in a glass pitcher and muddle them. Add the boiling water and tea bags and steep for 30 minutes.

2. Add the bourbon and sugar and stir until the sugar has dissolved. Chill the tea in the refrigerator for 3 hours and serve over ice in highball glasses.

APPLE PIE MOONSHINE PUNCH

This can be served hot or cold in a punch bowl. Either way, it's perfect for a crisp fall day.

5 cups apple cider

1 cup moonshine

½ cup brown sugar

4 cinnamon sticks

2 cored and diced apples

1. Place all of the ingredients in a slow cooker and warm it over low heat until the flavor has developed to your liking, about 2 hours.

2. If serving hot, ladle the punch into mugs and enjoy. If serving cold, transfer the punch to a container and chill it in the refrigerator. Serve over ice in rocks glasses.

APPLE PIE MOONSHINE PUNCH,
SEE PAGE 197

YIELD: **4 SERVINGS**

ACTIVE TIME: **1 HOUR**

TOTAL TIME: **25 HOURS**

RECIPE COURTESY OF CHEF MARCOS SIERRA
PAIRINGS COURTESY OF WILLIAM GEOGHEGAN

VEAL SHANKS WITH PEARS

If you have a large crowd, this also works well as a small plate. Pair with DYC 15 Year Old Whisky or the Temporis cocktail using it (see opposite page). The fruity, full-bodied DYC 15 provides a lovely bit of contrast to the veal.

5 lbs. suckling veal shanks

Salt and pepper, to taste

2 onions, chopped

2 carrots, peeled and chopped

1 garlic clove, chopped

3 sprigs of fresh rosemary

3 sprigs of fresh thyme

½ cup red wine

½ cup Chicken Stock (see page 245)

½ cup water

½ cup sugar

Pinch of fresh lemon thyme

3 San Juan pears

1. Season the veal shanks with salt and pepper and let them rest for 45 minutes.

2. Preheat a sous vide machine to 150°F. Place the veal shanks, onions, carrots, garlic, rosemary, thyme, red wine, and stock in a vacuum bag and seal it. Sous vide the veal shanks for 24 hours.

3. Place the remaining ingredients in a saucepan and cook them over low heat until the pears are very tender, about 45 minutes, stirring occasionally. Remove the pan from heat and let it cool to room temperature. Store the pears and the syrup in the refrigerator overnight.

4. Remove the pears from the refrigerator and let them come to room temperature. Remove the veal shanks from the sous vide machine and remove them from the bag. Strain the cooking liquid into a saucepan, bring it to a simmer, and reduce it until it is syrupy.

5. Drizzle the reduction over the veal shanks and serve the pears alongside them.

TEMPORIS

Courtesy of Roger Rueda
and George Restrepo

Yield: **1 Drink**
Active Time: **2 Minutes**
Total Time: **1 Month**

Get this decadent cocktail ready for
your holiday party.

Ingredients

1½ oz. DYC 15 Year Old Whisky

⅔ oz. Yellow Chartreuse

⅔ oz. chocolate liqueur

1 oz. pear juice

⅔ oz. Spiced Syrup (see page 255)

1. Place all of the ingredients in a
   mason jar and let the mixture age
   for at least 1 month.

2. Strain the cocktail over a large
   ice cube into a tumbler and enjoy.

DESSERTS

When it comes to the rule for the pairing events I have attended, sweets and desserts are the prevailing answer. They predominate across pairings with Scotch, Irish whiskey, bourbon, and other forms of American whiskey. Chocolate, cupcakes, pies, tarts, cookies, donuts, what have you, this is the go-to category of foods for pairing with whiskey, overshadowing everything else—even cheese and oysters.

YIELD: **1 PIE**

ACTIVE TIME: **45 MINUTES**

TOTAL TIME: **3 HOURS**

COURTESY OF MICHTER'S DISTILLERY

RYE APPLE PIE

This American classic needs subtle spice, a charge Michter's rye can happily meet.

3 lbs. Granny Smith or preferred baking apples, peels and cores removed, quartered

½ cup sugar, plus more for sprinkling

1 teaspoon kosher salt

½ teaspoon cinnamon

¾ cup Michter's US*1 Straight Rye

3 tablespoons unsalted butter, cut into small cubes

All-purpose flour, as needed

1 ball of Piecrust dough (see page 263)

1 teaspoon heavy cream

1. Preheat the oven to 375°F. Place the apples, sugar, salt, cinnamon, rye, and butter in a mixing bowl and toss to combine. Spread the mixture in an even layer on a rimmed baking sheet, place the pan in the oven, and bake until the apples are tender and the pan juices are syrupy, about 1 hour, stirring the apples every 20 minutes. Remove the apples from the oven and let them cool completely.

2. Dust a work surface with flour, place the pie dough on it, and roll it out to 13 inches. Place the crust in a 9-inch pie plate, fill the crust with the apples, pour the pan juices over the apples, and fold the piecrust over the filling. Place the pie in the refrigerator and chill for 15 minutes.

3. Preheat the oven to 350°F. Brush the piecrust with the heavy cream and sprinkle additional sugar over it. Place the pie in the oven and bake until the filling is bubbling and the crust is golden brown, 50 to 60 minutes.

4. Remove the pie from the oven and let it cool slightly before serving.

YIELD: **1 PIE**

ACTIVE TIME: **45 MINUTES**

TOTAL TIME: **3 HOURS**

COURTESY OF MELISSA KRUMBEIN, owner of Kitchen Thyme, Richmond, Virginia

DRUNKEN RAISIN & APPLE PIE

Fruity, floral, and slightly nutty, Roundstone Rye is right at home in the confectionary space.

For the Drunken Raisins

1 cup golden raisins

Catoctin Creek Roundstone Rye Whisky, as needed

For the Piecrust

1⅔ cups all-purpose flour, plus more as needed

8 teaspoons sugar

½ cup salted butter, chilled and cut into small pieces, plus more as needed

2 to 3 tablespoons bourbon

1 egg, beaten

For the Filling

2 tablespoons flambéed Catoctin Creek Roundstone Rye Whisky

6 Stayman apples, peels and cores removed, sliced ¼ inch thick

⅔ cup sugar

½ cup packed dark brown sugar

½ cup all-purpose flour

1 teaspoon cinnamon

⅛ teaspoon freshly grated nutmeg

⅛ teaspoon allspice

2 tablespoons unsalted butter, chilled and cut into small pieces

1. To prepare the drunken raisins, place the raisins in an airtight container and add the rye until the raisins are covered. Cover the container and let it rest at room temperature overnight. The next morning, carefully light the whisky on fire and let the flames dissipate on their own. Drain the raisins, reserve the liquid, and let the raisins cool.

2. To begin preparations for the piecrust, place the flour and sugar in a large mixing bowl and whisk to combine. Add the butter to the mixture and work it with your hands for 4 to 5 minutes, until it comes together in pea-sized clumps. Add 2 tablespoons of bourbon and work the mixture until it just comes together as a dough. If the mixture is too dry to come together, incorporate another tablespoon of bourbon. Shape the dough into a flat disk, cover it with plastic wrap, and chill the dough in the refrigerator for at least 30 minutes.

3. Preheat the oven to 425°F. To begin preparations for the filling, place all of the ingredients, except for the butter, in a mixing bowl and stir to combine. Set the mixture aside.

4. Cut the piecrust dough in half and place the pieces on a flour-dusted work surface. Roll each one out to fit a 9-inch pie plate. Coat the pie plate with butter, place one crust in the pie plate, and trim away any excess. Fill the crust with the apple mixture and dot the filling with the butter. Place the other piecrust over the filling, trim away any excess, and crimp the edge to seal. Cut a few slits in the top crust and brush it with the egg.

5. Place the pie in the oven and bake it until the crust is golden brown and the filling is bubbling, about 40 minutes. Remove the pie from the oven and let it cool on a wire rack before slicing and serving.

EVEN BETTER THAN EXTRACT

"It is generally accepted among cooking circles that alcohol is a flavor enhancer, so that is why people cook with wine," says Scott Harris, founder of Catoctin Creek Distillery. "The same goes for whiskey. What is interesting is that whiskey makes an interesting substitution for what one would usually use as vanilla extract. Vanilla extract is really nothing more than the compound vanillin in a tincture of alcohol. Whiskey, of course, is alcohol with vanillin derived from the barrel, plus the flavor of the grain. So, in things like pie, it's a natural."

YIELD: **1½ CUPS**

ACTIVE TIME: **15 MINUTES**

TOTAL TIME: **15 MINUTES**

COURTESY OF CHEF BRETT DILLON AND GARRISON BROTHERS DISTILLERY

BOURBON SALTED CARAMEL SAUCE

As you might expect, bourbon works beautifully in a caramel sauce, somehow managing to make it seem even more decadent.

1 cup Garrison Brothers Small Batch Bourbon

1 cup packed brown sugar

1 tablespoon kosher salt

2 tablespoons unsalted butter

1. Place the bourbon and brown sugar in a saucepan and warm the mixture over medium heat, whisking occasionally to dissolve the sugar. Cook the mixture for 10 minutes and remove the pan from heat.

2. Carefully add the salt and butter, stir until incorporated, and use the caramel as desired.

COURTESY OF MICHTER'S DISTILLERY

BLACKBERRY JAM BARS

A dram of Michter's US*1 Bourbon will partner beautifully with these delightful bars. Michter's bourbon has a golden raisin note, matching the blackberries without repeating.

½ cup unsalted butter, chilled and cut into small pieces, plus more as needed

2 cups pecans, toasted

1½ cups all-purpose flour

⅔ cup light brown sugar

½ teaspoon baking powder

½ teaspoon kosher salt

¾ cup blackberry jam

1. Preheat the oven to 350°F. Butter a square 9-inch baking dish and line it with parchment paper, leaving a 2-inch overhang on each side. Place the pecans, flour, brown sugar, baking powder, and salt in a food processor and pulse until the pecans are finely ground. Add the butter and pulse until the mixture is a crumbly dough. Remove 1½ cups of the mixture and set it aside.

2. Press the remaining dough into the baking dish, making sure it is even. Spread the jam over the crust and then sprinkle the reserved crumble over the jam.

3. Place the bars in the oven and bake until the jam is bubbling in the center and the topping is golden brown, about 45 minutes, rotating the pan halfway through. Remove the bars from the oven and let them cool completely before slicing and serving.

YIELD: **8 SERVINGS**

ACTIVE TIME: **15 MINUTES**

TOTAL TIME: **3 HOURS**

COURTESY OF CHEF STU PLUSH

CHOCOLATE BREAD PUDDING

If you don't have any day-old bread hanging around and are stuck using fresh bread, cut it into cubes and bake at 300°F for about 10 minutes to dry it out. Pair with Bardstown Bourbon Company Discovery Series #7. This choice is about offering a full-bodied pour that can stand up to this heavy brioche-based pudding, while offering a sweet and spicy contrast to its cocoa-driven character.

6 large eggs

1 cup sugar

1 tablespoon pure vanilla extract

Zest of 1 orange

2 tablespoons cocoa powder

2 cups milk

2 cups heavy cream

1 loaf of day-old Brioche (see page 241), cut into 1-inch cubes

1 cup dark chocolate chips

Caramel sauce (see page 209 for homemade), for serving

Vanilla ice cream, for serving

1. Place the eggs, sugar, vanilla, orange zest, and cocoa powder in a large mixing bowl and whisk until the mixture is smooth. Add the milk and heavy cream and whisk to combine. Add the bread and gently stir until the bread is evenly coated. Cover the bowl with plastic wrap, place it in the refrigerator, and let it chill for at least 1 hour.

2. Preheat the oven to 325°F. Coat a 13 x 9–inch baking dish with nonstick cooking spray. Bring water to a boil in a medium saucepan. Remove the bread mixture from the refrigerator, add the chocolate chips, and stir until they are evenly distributed. Pour the mixture into the baking dish and cover it with aluminum foil.

3. Place the baking dish in a large roasting pan. Pour the boiling water into the roasting pan until it reaches halfway up on the baking dish. Place the roasting pan in the oven and bake until the bread pudding is set, about 1 hour.

4. Remove the bread pudding from the oven, remove it from the roasting pan, and let it cool for 30 minutes. Serve with caramel and ice cream.

YIELD: **30 CARAMELS**

ACTIVE TIME: **20 MINUTES**

TOTAL TIME: **1 HOUR AND 30 MINUTES**

MILK CHOCOLATE & WHISKEY CARAMELS

Michter's US*1 American Whiskey has strong toffee, butterscotch, and caramel notes. In truth, it drinks a lot like a box of candies, complementing this treat nicely.

½ cup unsalted butter, divided into tablespoons, plus more as needed

½ cup water

½ cup corn syrup

¾ cup Michter's US*1 American Whiskey

2 cups sugar

½ cup heavy cream

Pinch of kosher salt

2 cups milk chocolate chips

1. Coat a square 9-inch baking dish with butter and line it with parchment paper, leaving a 2-inch overhang on each side of the dish. Place the water, corn syrup, ½ cup of whiskey, and the sugar in a saucepan and bring the mixture to a boil over medium-high heat, swirling the pan and brushing down the sides of the pot with a wet pastry brush, until the caramel is a deep amber, 10 to 15 minutes. Remove the pan from heat.

2. Carefully whisk in the butter, heavy cream, salt, and remaining whiskey. Place the pan over medium-high heat and bring the caramel to a boil, whisking frequently. Boil for 1 minute and remove the pan from heat.

3. Place the chocolate chips in a large, heatproof bowl. Pour the caramel over the chocolate chips and let the mixture sit for 2 minutes. Stir the mixture until smooth and well combined.

4. Pour the mixture into the baking dish, smoothing the top with a rubber spatula. Let the caramels cool completely.

5. Lift the caramels out of the baking dish, cut them into squares, and wrap them tightly in waxed paper.

CINNAMON & RYE ICE CREAM

A deliciously simple ice cream that doesn't require fancy gadgets.

1 (14 oz.) can of sweetened condensed milk

3 tablespoons Michter's US*1 Rye Whiskey

1½ teaspoons cinnamon

1 teaspoon pure vanilla extract

Pinch of kosher salt

2 cups heavy cream

1. Place the condensed milk, whiskey, cinnamon, vanilla, and salt in a mixing bowl and whisk until combined. Set the mixture aside.

2. Place the heavy cream in a large bowl and whip it until it holds stiff peaks.

3. Fold the whipped cream into the condensed milk mixture. Pour the mixture into a loaf pan or freezer-safe container. Cover with plastic wrap and freeze until the ice cream is firm, at least 5 hours.

DOUBLE CHOCOLATE &
CHERRY BROWNIES , SEE PAGE 218

YIELD: **20 BROWNIES**

ACTIVE TIME: **20 MINUTES**

TOTAL TIME: **1 HOUR AND 30 MINUTES**

DOUBLE CHOCOLATE & CHERRY BROWNIES

Just as it was a sound choice for accompanying the chocolate-and-caramel candies on page 213, Michter's US*1 American Whiskey goes hand in glove with these decadent brownies.

½ cup unsalted butter, plus more as needed

1 cup semisweet chocolate chips

1 cup sugar

½ cup packed light brown sugar

3 large eggs

1 teaspoon pure vanilla extract

½ teaspoon kosher salt

⅓ cup cocoa powder

¾ cup all-purpose flour

1 cup cocktail cherries, with their liquid

Confectioners' sugar, for dusting (optional)

1. Preheat the oven to 350°F and position a rack in the center of the oven. Coat a square 9-inch baking dish with butter and line it with parchment paper, leaving a 2-inch overhang on each side.

2. Fill a medium saucepan halfway with water and bring it to a simmer. Combine the butter and chocolate chips in a heatproof bowl and place the bowl over the simmering water. Warm the butter and chocolate chips, stirring occasionally, until the mixture is melted and smooth.

3. Remove the bowl from heat, add the sugars, and whisk until incorporated. Add the eggs, vanilla, and salt and whisk until incorporated.

4. Gradually add the cocoa powder and flour and fold the mixture until it comes together as a smooth batter. Add the cherries and their liquid and fold until incorporated.

5. Pour the batter into the baking dish, place it in the oven, and bake until the top of the brownies is starting to crack and a knife inserted into the center comes out with a few crumbs attached, 35 to 40 minutes.

6. Remove the brownies from the oven and let them cool on a wire rack. If desired, dust the brownies with confectioners' sugar before serving.

YIELD: **4 TO 6 SERVINGS**

ACTIVE TIME: **20 MINUTES**

TOTAL TIME: **1 HOUR**

PRE-MAPLE BRÛLÉE

A custard that one could submit to the torch, but is also lovely as is. For a pairing, go with George Dickel No. 12 Tennessee Whiskey.

4 cups heavy cream

1 cup egg yolks

¾ cup maple syrup

¼ cup sugar

1. Preheat the oven to 300°F. Place the cream in a saucepan and warm it over medium heat until bubbles form around the edge, 5 to 7 minutes. Remove the pan from heat.

2. Place the egg yolks in a mixing bowl, add the maple syrup and sugar, and beat until combined.

3. While whisking, pour the scalded cream into the egg yolk mixture.

4. Pour the custard into ramekins and place them in the oven. Bake until the custard has set, 25 to 30 minutes. Remove the ramekins from the oven and let the custards cool slightly before enjoying.

GEORGE DICKEL

Although always in the shadow of Jack Daniel's—the largest whiskey producer in both Tennessee and the world—Dickel can stand toe-to-toe with its rival when it comes to taste.

Dickel's No. 12 is the older, stronger cousin of its well-known No. 8 offering. It's the same production process and stock, just aged six to eight years and bottled at a higher proof. Its scent has a current of sweet butter smeared thickly across the top, and its palate carries a corn, honey, and caramel sweetness that is beautifully balanced by its complex spiciness, which carries notes of cinnamon, nutmeg, anise, and a little oak.

COURTESY OF MICHTER'S DISTILLERY

EGGNOG BARS

Everyone knows that few treats cap off the year quite like a bit of whiskey-spiked eggnog. Whipped cream and nutmeg make wonderful toppings for these bars.

For the Crust

4 tablespoons unsalted butter, melted and cooled to room temperature, plus more as needed

9 graham crackers

2 tablespoons sugar

Pinch of kosher salt

For the Cheesecake Layer

½ lb. cream cheese, softened

2 tablespoons sugar

Pinch of kosher salt

2 large eggs, at room temperature

1 teaspoon pure vanilla extract

For the Custard Layer

4 large egg yolks

1 (14 oz.) can of sweetened condensed milk

¼ cup eggnog

¼ cup Michter's US*1 bourbon

1 teaspoon pure vanilla extract

1. Preheat the oven to 350°F and position a rack in the center of the oven. Coat a square 9-inch baking dish with butter and line it with parchment paper, leaving a 2-inch overhang on each side. To prepare the crust, place the graham crackers, sugar, and salt in a food processor and pulse until the mixture is fine crumbs. Add the butter and pulse until the mixture looks like wet sand, scraping down the work bowl as needed. Press the mixture into the baking dish, place the dish in the oven, and bake until the crust is golden brown and fragrant, about 12 minutes. Remove the crust from the oven and set it aside.

2. To prepare the cheesecake layer, place the cream cheese, sugar, and salt in a mixing bowl and beat until combined. Add the eggs and vanilla and beat until incorporated. Reduce the oven's temperature to 325°F. Pour the cream cheese mixture over the crust, smooth the top, and place the baking dish in the oven. Bake until the cream cheese layer is just set, 10 to 12 minutes. Remove the baking dish from the oven and set it aside.

3. To prepare the custard layer, place the egg yolks in a mixing bowl and beat them until pale and slightly fluffy. Add the remaining ingredients and whisk until well combined. Pour the eggnog mixture over the hot cheesecake layer, return the baking dish to the oven, and bake until the eggnog layer is just set in the middle, 15 to 18 minutes.

4. Remove the bars from the oven and let them cool on a wire rack. Chill them in the refrigerator until they are firm, at least 2 hours.

5. Use the parchment to lift the bars out of the baking dish. Cut them into squares and enjoy.

COURTESY OF JOURNEYMAN DISTILLERY

FEATHERBONE TARTS

By utilizing two of its innovative spirits, Journeyman authors a one-of-a-kind confection.

For the Cherry Cocoa Nibs

1 cup cocoa nibs

⅓ cup Journeyman Pit-Spitter Cherry Rye Whiskey

1 cup sugar

For the Tarts

⅓ cup Journeyman Featherbone Bourbon Whiskey

½ cup sugar

¼ teaspoon kosher salt

3 tablespoons cornstarch

4 egg yolks

2 cups whole milk

2 tablespoons unsalted butter

12 miniature tart shells

1. To begin preparations for the cherry cocoa nibs, place the cocoa nibs and whiskey in a mason jar and let the cocoa nibs steep for 2 days.

2. Line a baking sheet with parchment paper. Drain the cocoa nibs and place them in a saucepan with the sugar. Warm the mixture over medium-high heat, stirring frequently, until the sugar has melted and is starting to crystalize. Continue stirring until the sugar has melted again and is coating the cocoa nibs. If sugar begins to harden too quickly, slowly add ⅓ cup of water to the pan and stir until the sugar loosens. Remove the pan from heat and spread the cocoa nibs on the baking sheet in an even layer, taking care to leave space between them. Be careful, as the cocoa nibs will be very hot.

3. To begin preparations for the tarts, place the whiskey in a saucepan and warm it over medium heat until it comes to a simmer. Remove the pan from heat and set it aside.

4. Prepare an ice bath. Combine the sugar, salt, and cornstarch in a mixing bowl, add the egg yolks and beat until the mixture is smooth, pale yellow, and fluffy. Whisk in the milk and pour the mixture into a saucepan and warm it over medium heat, whisking continually, until the custard is thick enough to coat the back of a wooden spoon. Scrape down the side of the saucepan with a rubber spatula, as this is where the eggs begin to overcook and curdle. Remove the pan from heat, whisk in the butter and whiskey, and place the custard in a mixing bowl. Place the bowl in the ice bath and stir until it is chilled.

5. Pour the custard into the tart shells, top with the cherry cocoa nibs, and enjoy.

129

YIELD: **1 CAKE**

ACTIVE TIME: **20 MINUTES**

TOTAL TIME: **2 HOURS AND 30 MINUTES**

COURTESY OF MICHTER'S DISTILLERY

SPICED SOUR CREAM BUNDT CAKE
WITH WHISKEY SYRUP

If you happen to have a cast-iron Bundt pan, this is a great opportunity to break it out, as it will lend this cake an eye-catching burnish.

1¼ cups unsalted butter, softened, plus more as needed

3 cups cake flour, plus more as needed

1½ cups packed light brown sugar

1⅓ cups sugar

1 teaspoon baking soda

1 teaspoon kosher salt

1 tablespoon cinnamon

6 large eggs, at room temperature

⅔ cup Michter's US*1 American Whiskey

1 tablespoon plus 1 teaspoon pure vanilla extract

1 cup sour cream, at room temperature

⅓ cup hot water (140°F)

Whipped cream, for serving

1. Preheat the oven to 350°F. Butter and flour a 12-cup Bundt pan and knock out any excess flour. Place the butter, brown sugar, and 1 cup of sugar in the work bowl of a stand mixer fitted with the paddle attachment and cream until light and fluffy, about 5 minutes.

2. Sift the flour, baking soda, salt, and cinnamon into a separate bowl.

3. Incorporate the eggs into the creamed butter one at a time, scraping down the work bowl as needed. Gradually add the flour mixture and beat until incorporated. Add ⅓ cup of whiskey, 1 tablespoon of vanilla, and the sour cream and beat until the mixture just comes together as a smooth batter. Pour the batter into the Bundt pan and smooth the top with a rubber spatula.

4. Place the pan in the oven and bake the cake until a knife inserted into the center comes out with a few crumbs attached, about 1 hour, rotating the pan halfway through.

5. Remove the cake from the oven and let it cool on a wire rack for 25 minutes.

6. Place the remaining sugar and the water in a saucepan and warm the mixture over medium heat, stirring to dissolve the sugar. Remove the pan from heat, stir in the remaining whiskey and vanilla, and let the syrup cool.

7. Turn the cake out of the pan and let it cool completely. Brush the cake with syrup every 10 minutes as it cools. Serve with whipped cream.

IRISH BROWNIES

Incorporating some Bushmills into the batter is akin to crushing up some toffee and dropping it in.

½ cup unsalted butter

2 eggs

1 cup sugar

½ cup all-purpose flour

⅓ cup cocoa powder

1 teaspoon pure vanilla extract

1½ oz. Bushmills Irish Whiskey

¼ teaspoon baking powder

½ teaspoon kosher salt

1. Preheat the oven to 350°F and coat a square 9-inch baking dish with nonstick cooking spray. Place the butter in a metal mixing bowl and melt it over low heat. Remove the bowl from heat, add the remaining ingredients, and whisk until the mixture comes together as a smooth batter.

2. Pour the batter into the baking dish, place it in the oven, and bake until the top of the brownies is starting to crack and a knife inserted into the center comes out with a few crumbs attached, 25 to 30 minutes.

3. Remove the brownies from the oven and let them cool completely before cutting them into squares.

JOURNEYMAN DISTILLERY

Michigan's Journeyman is a sweet-mash operation, and it uses only organically grown grains. As with other Midwestern distilleries, sourcing that grain isn't a problem: if Michigan doesn't happen to have what Journeyman needs, neighboring states can always provide it. For yeast, it relies on dry distiller's strains. Journeyman's production is centered on whiskey, with nine different expressions in its regular lineup, including rye, bourbon, wheat whiskey, American malt, and a four-grain whiskey. However, it has followed the path of being a distillery that does a little bit of everything. Thus, Journeyman also makes vodka, gin, rum, and brandy.

YIELD: **12 TARTS**

ACTIVE TIME: **30 MINUTES**

TOTAL TIME: **1 HOUR**

SILVER CROSS TARTS

By adding whiskey and buttermilk to the caramel, these sweet-and-spicy tarts become unforgettable.

For the Caramel

¼ cup Journeyman Silver Cross Whiskey

1 cup sugar

4 tablespoons unsalted butter

1 cup buttermilk

Pinch of kosher salt

For the Tarts

1 cup heavy cream

½ cup semisweet chocolate chips

¼ teaspoon cayenne pepper

⅛ teaspoon cinnamon

12 miniature tart shell

1. To begin preparations for the caramel, place the whiskey in a saucepan and warm it over medium heat until it comes to a simmer. Cook until the alcohol has been cooked off. Remove the pan from heat and set it aside.

2. Place the sugar in a deep saucepan and warm it over medium-low heat, swirling the pan occasionally, until it is melted. Remove the pan from heat and carefully stir in the butter. Add the buttermilk, salt, and whiskey and stir until combined. Set the caramel aside.

3. To begin preparations for the tarts, place the heavy cream in a small saucepan and bring to a gentle simmer. Place the chocolate chips in a mixing bowl, pour the cream over them, and let the mixture sit for 2 minutes. Stir the mixture until it is smooth.

4. Stir the cayenne and cinnamon into the ganache and then pour it into the tart shells. Top the tarts with the caramel and chill them in the refrigerator for 30 minutes before enjoying.

RECIPE COURTESY OF CHEF MARCOS SIERRA
PAIRING COURTESY OF WILLIAM GEOGHEGAN

SPANISH WHISKY CAKE

Nomad Outland Whisky, with its powerful notes of marzipan and raisins, matches the sweetness of this dessert, but it is its subtle current of licorice that will stand out.

½ cup water

½ cup sugar

1½ oz. Nomad Outland Whisky

1 large croissant

½ cup whipped cream

Caramel sauce (see page 209 for homemade), for serving

1. Place the water and sugar in a saucepan and warm it over medium heat, stirring to dissolve the sugar. Remove the pan from heat, carefully stir in the whiskey, and let the mixture cool slightly.

2. Place the croissant in the liquid and let it soak for 10 to 15 minutes, turning it occasionally.

3. Top the croissant with whipped cream, drizzle caramel over the top, and enjoy.

APPENDIX

DUCK CONFIT

6 duck legs

Salt, to taste

1 tablespoon extra-virgin olive oil

1. Pat the duck legs dry with paper towels and season them generously with salt. With the tip of a knife, gently poke the skin all around each leg. This will help release the fat as it renders. Let the legs rest at room temperature for at least 25 minutes.

2. Coat the bottom of a Dutch oven with the olive oil, add the duck legs, and set the oven to 285°F. Place the Dutch oven, uncovered, in the oven. You do not want to preheat the oven, as starting the duck at a low temperature allows its fat to render.

3. After 1½ hours, check the duck legs. They should be under a layer of duck fat and their skin should be getting crispy. If the legs aren't browned and crispy, let them cook longer. When the skin is starting to get crispy, raise the oven's temperature to 375°F and cook the duck legs for another 15 minutes.

4. Remove the pot from the oven, remove the duck legs from the fat, and let them rest for 10 minutes before serving.

YIELD: **2 CUPS**

ACTIVE TIME: **2 HOURS**

TOTAL TIME: **2 WEEKS**

SOURDOUGH STARTER

1 cup water, at room temperature, plus more daily

2 cups all-purpose flour, plus more daily

1. Place the water and flour in a large jar (the jar should be at least 1 quart). Combine the ingredients by hand, cover the jar, and let it stand in a sunny spot at room temperature for 24 hours.

2. Place 1 cup of the starter in a bowl, add 1 cup water and 2 cups all-purpose flour, and stir until thoroughly combined. Discard the remainder of the starter. Place the new mixture back in the jar and let it sit at room temperature for 24 hours. Repeat this process every day until you notice bubbles forming on the surface of the starter. This should take approximately 2 weeks. If the starter does not start to bubble after 2 weeks, feed it twice a day until it does.

3. Once the starter begins to bubble, it can be used in recipes. The starter can be stored at room temperature or in the refrigerator. If the starter is kept at room temperature, it must be fed once a day; if the starter is refrigerated, it can be fed every 3 to 6 days. The starter can be frozen for up to a month without feeding.

4. To feed the starter, place 1 cup of the starter in a bowl, add 1 cup flour and 1 cup water, and work the mixture with your hands until combined. Discard the remainder of the starter. It is recommended that you feed the starter 6 to 8 hours before making bread.

YIELD: **1 LOAF**

ACTIVE TIME: **20 MINUTES**

TOTAL TIME: **30 HOURS**

SOURDOUGH BREAD

1⅔ cups plus 1 teaspoon filtered water (78°F)

5 cups bread flour, plus more as needed

¾ cup Sourdough Starter (see page 235)

1½ teaspoons fine sea salt

1. Combine the 1⅔ cups water and the flour in a bowl and work the mixture until it just comes together as a dough. Cover the dough and let it rest for 30 minutes.

2. Add the Sourdough Starter, salt, and remaining water to the dough. Knead for 10 minutes, until the dough is smooth and elastic. Place the dough in a bowl, cover with plastic wrap, and store in a naturally warm place for 4 hours.

3. Place the dough on a flour-dusted work surface and fold the left side of the dough to the right, fold the right side of the dough to the left, and fold the bottom toward the top. Form the dough into a rough ball, return it to the bowl, cover with plastic wrap, and let the dough rest for 30 minutes.

4. After 30 minutes, place the ball of dough on a flour-dusted work surface and repeat the folds made in Step 3. Form the dough into a ball, dust it with flour, and place it in a bowl with the seam facing up. Cover the bowl and place it in the refrigerator overnight.

5. About 2 hours before you plan to bake, remove the bread from the refrigerator, place it on a square of parchment paper, and let it come to room temperature.

6. Preheat the oven to 500°F. Place a covered cast-iron Dutch oven in the oven as it warms.

7. Remove the Dutch oven from the oven and carefully lower the square of parchment paper with the ball of dough on it into the Dutch oven. Score the top of the dough with a very sharp knife or razor blade, making a long cut across the middle. Cover the Dutch oven, place it in the oven, and bake for 25 minutes.

8. Remove the lid from the Dutch oven, lower the oven's temperature to 480°F, and bake the bread until it is golden brown and sounds hollow when tapped, about 25 minutes.

9. Remove the bread from the oven and let it cool on a wire rack for 2 hours before slicing.

PITA BREAD

1 cup lukewarm water (90°F)

1 tablespoon active dry yeast

1 tablespoon sugar

1¾ cups all-purpose flour, plus more as needed

1 cup whole wheat flour

1 tablespoon kosher salt

1. In a large mixing bowl, combine the water, yeast, and sugar. Let the mixture sit until it starts to foam, about 15 minutes.

2. Add the flours and salt and work the mixture until it comes together as a smooth dough. Cover the bowl with a linen towel and let it rise for about 15 minutes.

3. Preheat the oven to 500°F and place a baking stone on the floor of the oven.

4. Divide the dough into eight pieces and form them into balls. Place the balls on a flour-dusted work surface, press them down, and roll them until they are about ¼ inch thick.

5. Working with one pita at a time, place the pita on the baking stone and bake until it is puffy and brown, about 8 minutes. Remove from the oven and serve warm or at room temperature.

PITA BREAD,
SEE PAGE 237

YIELD: **18 X 13–INCH FOCACCIA**
ACTIVE TIME: **45 MINUTES**
TOTAL TIME: **4 HOURS**

FOCACCIA

For the Poolish

3¼ cups water

2 tablespoons active dry yeast

½ cup sugar

½ cup plus 2 tablespoons extra-virgin olive oil

For the Dough

28 oz. bread flour

20 oz. all-purpose flour

2 tablespoons chopped fresh rosemary

1 tablespoon chopped fresh thyme

2 tablespoons chopped fresh basil

3 tablespoons kosher salt

1½ teaspoons black pepper

1½ cups extra-virgin olive oil, plus more as needed

1 cup freshly shaved Parmesan cheese

1. To prepare the poolish, place all of the ingredients in a mixing bowl and whisk to combine. Cover the bowl with a linen towel and let it sit at room temperature for 30 minutes.

2. To begin preparations for the dough, place the poolish in the work bowl of a stand mixer fitted with the dough hook. Add all the remaining ingredients, except for the olive oil and Parmesan, and work the mixture on low for 1 minute. Raise the speed to medium and knead the mixture until it comes together as a smooth dough, about 5 minutes. Cover the bowl with a linen towel and let the dough rise until it has doubled in size.

3. Preheat the oven to 350°F.

4. Coat an 18 x 13–inch sheet pan with olive oil and place the dough on the pan. Use your fingers to gradually stretch the dough until it fills the entire pan and is as even as possible. If the dough is difficult to stretch, let it rest for 10 minutes before resuming.

5. Cover the dough with plastic wrap and let it rise at room temperature until it has doubled in size.

6. Use your fingertips to gently press down on the dough and make dimples all over it. The dimples should go about halfway down. Drizzle about 1 cup of olive oil over the focaccia and sprinkle the Parmesan on top.

7. Place the focaccia in the oven and bake until it is a light golden brown, 20 to 30 minutes.

8. Remove the focaccia from the oven and brush it generously with olive oil. Let it cool slightly before slicing and serving.

BRIOCHE

For the Sponge

½ cup milk, warmed

4½ teaspoons active dry yeast

2 tablespoons honey

4 oz. bread flour

For the Dough

5 eggs, 1 beaten

2 oz. sugar

1 lb. bread flour

2 teaspoons kosher salt

1 cup unsalted butter, softened

1. To prepare the sponge, place all of the ingredients in the work bowl of a stand mixer. Cover with plastic wrap and let the mixture sit until it starts to bubble, about 30 minutes.

2. To begin preparations for the dough, add the 4 unbeaten eggs to the sponge and whisk until incorporated.

3. Add the sugar, flour, and salt, fit the mixer with the dough hook, and knead the mixture on low speed for 5 minutes.

4. Over the course of 2 minutes, add the butter a little at a time with the mixer running. When all of the butter has been added, knead the mixture on low for 5 minutes.

5. Raise the speed to medium and knead the dough until it begins to pull away from the side of the work bowl, about 6 minutes. Cover the bowl with a kitchen towel, place the dough in a naturally warm spot, and let it rise until it has doubled in size, about 1 hour.

6. Preheat the oven to 350°F. Coat two 8 x 4–inch loaf pans with nonstick cooking spray.

7. Divide the dough into two equal pieces and flatten each one into a rectangle the width of a loaf pan. Tuck in the sides to form the dough into loaf shapes and place one in each pan, seam side down.

8. Cover the pans with plastic wrap and let the dough rise until it has crested over the tops of the pans.

9. Brush the loaves with the beaten egg, place them in the oven, and bake until golden brown, 35 to 45 minutes. The loaves should reach an internal temperature of 200°F.

10. Remove the loaves from the oven, place them on a wire rack, and let them cool before enjoying.

BRIOCHE,
SEE PAGE 241

CORNBREAD

½ cup honey

1½ cups unsalted butter, softened

3 cups plus 3¾ tablespoons all-purpose flour

½ lb. cornmeal

1 tablespoon plus 1 teaspoon baking powder

1 tablespoon kosher salt

1 cup sugar

4 eggs

2 cups milk

1. Preheat the oven to 350°F. Coat a large cast-iron skillet with nonstick cooking spray.

2. Place the honey and one-third of the butter in a small saucepan and warm the mixture over medium heat until the butter has melted. Whisk to combine and set the mixture aside.

3. Place the flour, cornmeal, baking powder, and salt in a mixing bowl and whisk to combine. Set the mixture aside.

4. In the work bowl of a stand mixer fitted with the paddle attachment, cream the remaining butter and the sugar on medium until light and fluffy, about 5 minutes. Add the eggs and beat until incorporated. Add the dry mixture, reduce the speed to low, and beat until the mixture comes together as a smooth batter. Gradually add the milk and beat until incorporated.

5. Pour the batter into the skillet and gently tap it on the counter to remove any air bubbles and evenly distribute the batter. Place the pan in the oven and bake until a cake tester inserted into the center of the cornbread comes out clean, 25 to 30 minutes.

6. Remove the pan from the oven and place it on a wire rack. Brush the cornbread with the honey butter and serve it warm.

YIELD: **8 CUPS**

ACTIVE TIME: **20 MINUTES**

TOTAL TIME: **6 HOURS**

CHICKEN STOCK

7 lbs. chicken bones, rinsed

4 cups chopped yellow onions

2 cups chopped carrots

2 cups chopped celery

3 garlic cloves, crushed

3 sprigs of fresh thyme

1 teaspoon black peppercorns

1 bay leaf

1. Place the chicken bones in a stockpot and cover with cold water. Bring to a simmer over medium-high heat and use a ladle to skim off any impurities that rise to the surface.

2. Add the vegetables, thyme, peppercorns, and bay leaf, reduce the heat to low, and simmer for 5 hours, skimming to remove any impurities that rise to the surface.

3. Strain, allow to cool slightly, and transfer the stock to the refrigerator. Leave uncovered and let the stock cool completely. Remove the layer of fat and cover. The stock will keep in the refrigerator for 3 to 5 days, and in the freezer for up to 3 months.

YIELD: **8 CUPS**

ACTIVE TIME: **20 MINUTES**

TOTAL TIME: **6 HOURS**

BEEF STOCK

7 lbs. beef bones, rinsed

4 cups chopped yellow onions

2 cups chopped carrots

2 cups chopped celery

3 garlic cloves, crushed

3 sprigs of fresh thyme

1 teaspoon black peppercorns

1 bay leaf

1. Place the beef bones in a stockpot and cover with cold water. Bring to a simmer over medium-high heat and use a ladle to skim off any impurities that rise to the surface.

2. Add the remaining ingredients, reduce the heat to low, and simmer for 5 hours, occasionally skimming to remove any impurities that rise to the surface.

3. Strain, let the stock cool slightly, and transfer to the refrigerator. Leave uncovered and let cool completely. Remove the layer of fat and cover. The stock will keep in the refrigerator for 3 to 5 days, and in the freezer for up to 3 months.

YIELD: **4 CUPS**

ACTIVE TIME: **5 MINUTES**

TOTAL TIME: **1 HOUR AND 5 MINUTES**

HAM STOCK

¾ lb. ham

6 cups water

2 garlic cloves, minced

1 onion, chopped

1 bay leaf

1 sprig of fresh thyme

1. Place all of the ingredients in a stockpot and bring to a boil.

2. Reduce the heat and simmer the stock for 1 hour.

3. Strain the stock through a fine sieve and chill it in the refrigerator.

YIELD: **6 CUPS**

ACTIVE TIME: **20 MINUTES**

TOTAL TIME: **3 HOURS**

VEGETABLE STOCK

2 tablespoons extra-virgin olive oil

2 large leeks, trimmed and rinsed well

2 large carrots, peeled and sliced

2 celery stalks, sliced

2 large yellow onions, sliced

3 garlic cloves, unpeeled, smashed

2 sprigs of fresh parsley

2 sprigs of fresh thyme

1 bay leaf

8 cups water

½ teaspoon black peppercorns

Salt, to taste

1. Place the olive oil and the vegetables in a large stockpot and cook over low heat until the liquid they release has evaporated. This will allow the flavor of the vegetables to become concentrated.

2. Add the garlic, parsley, thyme, bay leaf, water, peppercorns, and salt. Raise the heat to high and bring to a boil. Reduce heat so that the stock simmers and cook for 2 hours, while skimming to remove any impurities that float to the surface.

3. Strain through a fine sieve, let the stock cool slightly, and place in the refrigerator, uncovered, to chill. Remove the fat layer and cover. The stock will keep in the refrigerator for 3 to 5 days, and in the freezer for up to 3 months.

YIELD: **1 CUP**

ACTIVE TIME: **5 MINUTES**

TOTAL TIME: **5 MINUTES**

HORSERADISH CREAM

2 tablespoons grated fresh horseradish

2 teaspoons white wine vinegar

½ teaspoon Dijon mustard

1 cup heavy cream

Salt and pepper, to taste

1. Combine the horseradish, vinegar, mustard, and ¼ cup of the cream in a mixing bowl.

2. Lightly whip the remaining cream and then fold this into the horseradish mixture. Season to taste and refrigerate until ready to serve.

CRISPY CHICKEN SKINS

Skin from 2 large chicken thighs

Salt, to taste

1. Preheat the oven to 400°F. Lay the chicken skins on a cutting board, top down, and use a sharp paring knife to scrape off any excess fat and meat.

2. Stretch the skins out on a parchment-lined baking sheet and season them with salt.

3. Lay a second sheet of parchment paper over the chicken skins and then place another baking sheet on top. Place the baking sheets in the oven and bake the chicken skins until golden and crispy, about 10 minutes.

4. Remove the crispy skins from the oven and let them cool before using.

YIELD: **1½ CUPS**

ACTIVE TIME: **10 MINUTES**

TOTAL TIME: **1 HOUR**

SIMPLE SYRUP

1 cup sugar

1 cup water

1. Place the sugar and water in a small saucepan and bring to a boil, stirring to dissolve the sugar.

2. Remove the pan from heat and let the syrup cool completely before using or storing.

VANILLA SYRUP

1 cup water

1 cup sugar

3 vanilla beans, split

1. Place the ingredients in a saucepan and bring to a boil, stirring to dissolve the sugar.

2. Remove the pan from heat, let the syrup cool completely, and strain before using or storing.

YIELD: **1½ CUPS**

ACTIVE TIME: **10 MINUTES**

TOTAL TIME: **1 HOUR**

SPICED SYRUP

1 cup water

1 cup sugar

3 cinnamon sticks

5 whole cloves

5 allspice berries

3 cardamom pods

1. Place all of the ingredients in a small saucepan and bring to a boil over medium heat, stirring to dissolve the sugar.

2. Remove the pan from heat, let the syrup cool completely, and strain it before using or storing.

YIELD: **1¼ CUPS**

ACTIVE TIME: **5 MINUTES**

TOTAL TIME: **5 MINUTES**

CITRIC ACID SOLUTION

9 oz. water

1 oz. citric acid

1. Place the ingredients in a mason stir and stir until thoroughly combined. Use immediately or store in the refrigerator.

YIELD: ½ CUP

ACTIVE TIME: **10 MINUTES**

TOTAL TIME: **25 MINUTES**

BALSAMIC GLAZE

1 cup balsamic vinegar

¼ cup brown sugar

1. Place the vinegar and sugar in a small saucepan and bring the mixture to a boil.

2. Reduce the heat to medium-low and simmer for 8 to 10 minutes, stirring frequently, until the mixture has thickened.

3. Remove the pan from heat and let the glaze cool for 15 minutes before using.

YIELD: **4 TO 6 SERVINGS**

ACTIVE TIME: **30 MINUTES**

TOTAL TIME: **2 HOURS AND 30 MINUTES**

COLLARD GREENS

2 tablespoons extra-virgin olive oil

1 onion, diced

½ lb. smoked ham, diced

4 garlic cloves, diced

3 lbs. collard greens, stems removed, chopped

2 cups Vegetable Stock (see page 248)

¼ cup apple cider vinegar

1 tablespoon brown sugar

1 teaspoon red pepper flakes

1. Place the olive oil in a Dutch oven and warm it over medium-high heat. Add the onion and cook, stirring occasionally, until it is translucent, about 3 minutes.

2. Add the ham and cook the mixture over medium heat until the ham starts to brown. Stir in the remaining ingredients, cover the pot, and braise the collard greens until they are extremely tender, about 2 hours. Check on the collard greens every so often and add water if all of the liquid evaporates, so the greens do not burn.

YIELD: **4 CUPS**

ACTIVE TIME: **15 MINUTES**

TOTAL TIME: **45 MINUTES**

TOMATO SAUCE

2 tablespoons avocado oil

1 large garlic clove, chopped

1 teaspoon grated fresh ginger

1 cinnamon stick

1 (28 oz.) can of chopped San Marzano tomatoes, with their liquid

½ teaspoon cumin

¼ teaspoon coriander

⅛ teaspoon cayenne pepper

1. Place the avocado oil in a large saucepan and warm it over medium heat. Add the garlic and ginger and cook, stirring frequently, until fragrant, about 1 minute.

2. Add the cinnamon stick and cook for 30 seconds. Add the remaining ingredients and bring the sauce to a boil.

3. Reduce the heat and simmer the sauce until the flavor has developed to your liking, about 30 minutes.

4. Remove the cinnamon stick from the sauce and use as desired.

APPLE BUTTER

3 cups brandy

5 lbs. apples

½ cup maple syrup

¼ cup brown sugar

1 teaspoon kosher salt

½ teaspoon cinnamon

¼ teaspoon coriander

¼ teaspoon whole cloves

¼ teaspoon freshly grated nutmeg

1. Place the brandy in a saucepan and warm it over medium-high heat until it has reduced by half. Remove the pan from heat and set it aside.

2. Make sure to wash the apples thoroughly. Cut them into quarters, place them in a stockpot, and cover with cold water. Bring to a boil over medium-high heat and then reduce the heat so that the apples simmer. Cook until tender, about 15 minutes, and drain.

3. Preheat the oven to 225°F. Run the apples through a food mill and catch the pulp in a mixing bowl. Add the reduced brandy and the remaining ingredients, stir to combine, and transfer to a baking dish.

4. Place the baking dish in the oven and bake the apple mixture, stirring every 10 minutes, until all of the excess liquid has evaporated, about 1 to 1½ hours.

5. Remove the baking dish from the oven, transfer the mixture to a food processor, and puree until smooth.

YIELD: **2 PIECRUSTS**

ACTIVE TIME: **15 MINUTES**

TOTAL TIME: **2 HOURS AND 15 MINUTES**

PIECRUSTS

1 cup unsalted butter, cubed

2½ cups all-purpose flour, plus more as needed

½ teaspoon kosher salt

4 teaspoons sugar

½ cup ice water

1. Transfer the butter to a small bowl and place it in the freezer.

2. Place the flour, salt, and sugar in a food processor and pulse a few times until combined.

3. Add the chilled butter and pulse until the mixture is crumbly, consisting of pea-sized clumps.

4. Add the water and pulse until the mixture comes together as a dough.

5. Place the dough on a flour-dusted work surface and fold it over itself until it is a ball. Divide the dough in two and flatten each piece into a 1-inch-thick disk. Cover each piece completely with plastic wrap and place the dough in the refrigerator for at least 2 hours before rolling it out to fit your pie plate.

METRIC CONVERSIONS

US Measurement	Approximate Metric Liquid Measurement	Approximate Metric Dry Measurement
1 teaspoon	5 ml	5 g
1 tablespoon or ½ ounce	15 ml	14 g
1 ounce or ⅛ cup	30 ml	29 g
¼ cup or 2 ounces	60 ml	57 g
⅓ cup	80 ml	76 g
½ cup or 4 ounces	120 ml	113 g
⅔ cup	160 ml	151 g
¾ cup or 6 ounces	180 ml	170 g
1 cup or 8 ounces or ½ pint	240 ml	227 g
1½ cups or 12 ounces	350 ml	340 g
2 cups or 1 pint or 16 ounces	475 ml	454 g
3 cups or 1½ pints	700 ml	680 g
4 cups or 2 pints or 1 quart	950 ml	908 g

INDEX

ACKNOWLEDGMENTS

Depending on how one counts these things, *The Whiskey Cookbook* is either my eighth or ninth book. Although it is cliché to modestly declare in the Acknowledgments that "I couldn't have done it alone," in this instance I feel that to be an accurate way to put it. This book might not even exist, and certainly would not be what it is, were it not for the contributions and aid of so many people.

Topping that list are my contributors: Emma Briones, Sarah Jeltema, and Alexander Lopez-Wilson. I usually dread collaborations, because entering into one is often asking for trouble. But Emma, Sarah, and Alex were refreshingly easy to work with. I asked, and received more than I could have ever hoped for: they were eager to help, delivered on what they promised, and brought welcome regional diversity to the recipes and pairings.

Next are the folks in the whiskey industry who helped me. Down in Texas, Dan Garrison and Jack MacDonald were very generous. Lillie Pierson was both organized and supportive. Turn to a random page, and more than likely the fingerprints of one of these folks will be on it.

Finally, there are those who connected me with many of the chefs referenced here. Although their individual contributions were small, as a group they became the foundation which I built upon: Kayla Catherwood, Alexis Fraser, Ron Gomes, Tracy Green, Meredith Grelli, Caroline Knop, Izzy Hutnik, Holly McKnight, Shane Pirie, Richard Plantania, Colin Staunton, and Nicole Stipp.

CONTRIBUTORS

Richard Thomas

Richard's love of cooking began through working in mom-and-pop restaurants as a teenager, and although it hasn't been a professional pursuit since college, he continued to formally study food in Argentina, Cambodia, India, Malaysia, Mexico, Portugal, Thailand, and Vietnam. He is also the owner and editor of The Whiskey Reviewer website, has written or contributed to four other books about drink, and penned innumerable articles about both food and whiskey.

Emma Briones

Emma co-founded the blog Todo Whisky in 2012, which has become a reference for the Spanish community worldwide. She also writes for The Whiskey Reviewer and serves as a judge for the World Whiskies Awards. She's been awarded Highly Commended Communicator of the Year 2021 (RoW) by the Icons of Whisky Awards.

Sarah Jeltema

Sarah is a well-known whiskey influencer, blogger, and educator. Aside from running the website Whisky Nomad, she also co-founded the First Responder Whiskey Society, is President of Women Who Whiskey San Diego, and is the Assistant Director of Whiskey at the Museum of Distilled Spirits. She is a Certified Specialist of Spirits and has traveled to more than 25 countries, visiting distilleries and restaurants across the world.

Alexander Lopez-Wilson

Born in the Wyoming mountains, Alex grew up working in the hospitality world of Jackson Hole and Park City. This background and lifelong love of history and research have turned an early appreciation for wine into an intrepid career. With a focus that has tended towards education, Alex loves looking for the next trends in wine and spirits so that he can bring the best value to the consumer. Alex's background is in wine, but has begun to focus more about the spirits side, studying to become a Certified Specialist of Spirits.

ABOUT CIDER MILL PRESS
BOOK PUBLISHERS

Good ideas ripen with time. From seed to harvest, Cider Mill Press brings
fine reading, information, and entertainment together between the covers of its
creatively crafted books. Our Cider Mill bears fruit twice a year,
publishing a new crop of titles each spring and fall.

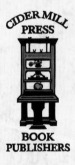

"Where Good Books Are Ready for Press"

Visit us online at
cidermillpress.com

or write to us at
PO Box 454
12 Spring St.
Kennebunkport, Maine 04046